I0486564

Sell, Sell, Sell

A Daily Prescription to Successful Sales

By

Smiley Anders

authorHOUSE™

1663 LIBERTY DRIVE, SUITE 200
BLOOMINGTON, INDIANA 47403
(800) 839-8640
WWW.AUTHORHOUSE.COM

© 2005 Smiley Anders. All Rights Reserved.

No part of this book may be reproduced, stored in a retrieval system, or transmitted by any means without the written permission of the author.

First published by AuthorHouse 09/26/05

ISBN: 1-4208-8196-5 (sc)

Library of Congress Control Number: 2005907989

Printed in the United States of America
Bloomington, Indiana

This book is printed on acid-free paper.

ACKNOWLEDGEMENT

This is a daily motivational and inspirational guide based on the accumulated written notes of Stanley L. Heine about his life in sales in Louisiana and Southern Mississippi. Although he worked as a sales manager for many years, Stanley Heine gained his early experience in selling as a "drummer." A "drummer" is a sales maker who travels and sells store-to-store, town-to-town. It was here that he honed the basic skills of selling. In describing sales makers, the term "consummate" is often used. Its meaning is, "to perfect." To perfect selling was Stanley Heine's passion. In his capacity as Sales Manager, he was constantly conducting sales meetings as part of his employment. His personal notes for his sales presentations were normally hand written, although a few were typed if they were to be handouts. At his death at 92, in excess of 500 sheets of notes about salesmanship and moral wisdom were found and cataloged by his son-in-law, Sam Gallo. Sam's corporate career involved managing sales divisions, and he could not bring himself to destroying Stanley Heine's accumulated sales notes. So, Sam brought Stanley Heine's papers to me to review with the suggestion that I author a book about selling using the Heine notes as source material for a book. After reviewing the papers, it was an easy decision to author the book, especially since my father was also in sales during the same period of time.

Mr. Heine talks about men pretty much exclusively, because in his day, virtually all the sales forces were composed of men; even in real estate, a profession dominated by women today. I didn't change his references to men because this was what he said and it was true of the time he was working.

Stanley Heine, my father, and others of their time, are a vanishing, perhaps vanished breed. I have done my best at transforming the Heine notes into a very readable guide to "old-fashioned" honest salesmanship. From a time when integrity was valued more than money. These days it would be a most valuable message for everyone in business.

Smiley Anders

INTRODUCTION

I am pleased that the author of this book, Smiley Anders, has given me the opportunity to write this introduction. It allows me to describe some background about my decision to contact Smiley Anders when I first came upon the sales notes of Stanley Heine, my father-in-law.

There is a sales axiom, "that nothing happens until something is sold." These words are greatly respected by executives charged with managing business enterprises. Having lived that leadership role for some 40 plus years, I cannot tell you the excruciating distress of witnessing poor sales figures, or the extreme joy of good ones. Until one is placed in a leadership role that forces one to personally experience these two outer limits of sales results, those lacking in it will never truly appreciate their business' sales force. Those in the accounting department may gripe that sales persons make too much money. Listen up. There would be no accounting tasks to perform until something is sold. And the song goes on.

Nothing, nothing, happens until something is sold!

I have concern about where business is heading in the future as it generates a mentality that has us becoming a "self-sell" society. "Look it up on the Internet and order it," is today's message. Do it yourself. And because we have become a "self-sell" society, sales persons are fast becoming irritants in our lives. Yes, there are abuses, i.e., phone calls at suppertime, and unwanted faxes, or spam emails. Yet I ask you this question. Don't you find it more difficult lately to make intelligent purchasing decisions? I do. When was the last time a sales person explained a product to you in words that helped you understand how that product would perform, or meet your expectations? Better yet, can you even find a sales person? Retail stores have taken on the "self-sell" mentality. "Take it off the rack, or shelves, and bring it to the cashier," is another of today's messages. Do it yourself!

While I have concern about all the erosion of pure selling , I've done very little to reverse its course. Yet, Stanley Heine had concern, and he attempted to reverse the course by instructing and leading sales personnel all of his life. He constantly made notes about selling, and for reasons best known to himself, he kept his notes, hundreds of pages of them.

Upon his death, I was charged with the responsibility of winding up his modest estate. It was then that I found his notes. Having the mindset that I described about me above, I could not bring myself to destroy his notes. There was a voice within me that kept saying, "Sam, you can't do it. Somewhere there is a person that Stanley's sales guidance can help be a better sales person. And what greater testament can his life reflect than to have his sales guidance carry on in book form."

Stanley Heine's papers were essentially notes to be used in his daily work. But, here is where we all benefit. Smiley Anders is a professional writer who has taken the Heine notes and presented them in an easily understandable form. I owe a debt of gratitude to him for taking on the job of writing this book. I could not have done it, no matter how much the effort.

So, here we are. This book is meant to be used. It was published in paperback and in a 5 by 8 inch size on purpose. The colors, red, white, and blue, on the cover are to remind us that in great measure this country's prosperity came through sales that made it happen. This is the kind of book to be in one's desk drawer, attaché' case, carry-on luggage to be read on an airplane, lent to others, in other words, used, beat up, scribbled in.

Last, Stanley Heine's work was meant to be private, thus there may be cases where attribution of content is not known. If, and when it is known, attribution will be shown.

Sam Gallo

A PHILOSOPHY OF LIFE: BECOMING A BETTER PERSON TO BECOME A BETTER SALESMAN.

TO S.L. HEINE, SR., SELLING WAS MORE THAN MOVING GOODS. IT CALLED FOR A SPECIAL PERSON, WITH SPECIAL VALUES AND QUALITIES. SOME OF HIS THOUGHTS ON LIFE:

WHAT IS MATURITY?

MATURITY IS THE SECRET OF A WELL ADJUSTED AND HAPPY LIFE. IT HELPS MAN TO CONTROL HIS BASIC IMPULSES AND DESIRES AND TO DIRECT THEM INTO CHANNELS WHERE THEY DO THE MOST GOOD.

MATURE PERSONS KNOW HOW TO COMPROMISE WITH LIFE. THEY ARE HAPPY AND WORK HARMONIOUSLY WITH OTHER BECAUSE THEY ARE ABLE TO ADJUST TO MANY SITUATIONS. IMMATURITY AND PREJUDICE GO HAND IN HAND. IT TAKES A WELL ROUNDED PERSON TO GIVE AND TAKE OR TO ACCEPT CONTROVERSIAL CHANGES WHEN THE OVERALLADVANTAGES ARE OBVIOUS.

AN ESSAY ON LOYALTY

REMEMBER THIS. IF YOU WORK FOR A MAN, IN HEAVEN'S NAME, WORK FOR HIM. IF HE PAYS YOUR WAGES THAT SUPPLY YOU FOOD, WORK FOR HIM, SPEAK WELL OF HIM: STAND BY HIM AND STAND BY THE COMPANY HE REPRESENTS. IF PUT TO A TEST, AN

OUNCE OF LOYALTY IS WORTH A POUND OF CLEVERNESS...

(by another, but unknown.)

DO FOR OTHERS

STOP THINKING ABOUT YOURSELF; LIGHTEN YOUR OWN LOAD BY DOING SOMETHING FOR SOMEONE ELSE. IT WILL KEEP YOU FROM MORBID WORRY AND FEAR...IT'S THE BEST MEDICINE. THERE IS ONLY ONE WAY TO HAPPINESS AND THAT IS TO CEASE WORRYING ABOUT THINGS WHICH ARE BEYOND OUR WILL. BE NOT SIMPLY GOOD; BE GOOD FOR SOMETHING.

CHANNELS OF CHALLENGE

THE THOUGHT THAT ONE MUST ALWAYS SUCCEED IS A DEVASTATING HINDRANCE TO SPIRITUAL DEVELOPMENT. A PERSON BOUND BY THE NECESSITY OF SUCCEEDING IN EVERY ENDEAVOR NEVER KNOWS THE FREEDOM OF ADVENTURE. HE NEVER TRIES THAT OF WHICH HE CANNOT BE ABSOLUTELY CERTAIN. THUS HE MISSES THE GLORY OF STEPPING OUT INTO THE UNKNOWN AND THE UNCERTAIN.

LIFE IS NOW

WHATEVER IT OFFERS, LITTLE OR MUCH, LIFE IS NOW - THIS DAY - THIS HOUR. ENJOY YOUR LIFE WITHOUT COMPARING IT WITH THAT OF OTHERS.

NUTS AND BOLTS: THE MECHANICS OF SELLING

S.L. HEINE, SR. INSTRUCTED A GENERATION OF SALES PEOPLE ON THE ART OF SELLING, TELLING THEM IN GREAT DETAIL HOW TO PRESENT THE PRODUCT, GAIN THE BUYER'S TRUST, AND CLOSE THE DEAL.

A NATURAL-BORN SALESMAN?

WHEN ANYONE SAYS THAT A MAN IS A NATURAL-BORN SALESMAN, HE IS PERPETUATING A MYTH. THE DESIGNATION IMPLIES THAT THE ABILITY TO SELL IS PRIMARILY A NATIVE ONE; THAT THE PERSON IS A SPELLBINDER.

ACTUALLY, ANY NORMAL PERSON INTERESTED IN SELLING CAN LEARN, AND HAVING LEARNED, CAN PRACTICE SELLING SUCCESSFULLY.

THE SPELL-BINDER WHO CANNOT ANSWER TECHNICAL QUESTIONS IS QUITE LIKELY TO LOSE THE ORDER TO A COMPETING SALESMAN WHO MAY HAVE A LESS GLIB TONGUE BUT CAN DEMONSTRATE THE WORTH AND APPLICATION OF HIS PRODUCT...

KNOW YOUR PRODUCT

A SUCCESSFUL SALESMAN'S KNOWLEDGE MUST EXTEND FAR BEYOND THE MERE SELLING OF COFFEE AND THE INSTALLATION

OF COFFEE MACHINES AND URNS. HE MUST MAKE HIMSELF COMPETENT TO ADVISE PROSPECTS ON MATTERS PUZZLING THEM ABOUT COFFEE AND COFFEE BREWING PROBLEMS. BE DETERMINED TO BECOME A PROFESSIONAL SALESMAN; LEARN ALL THAT YOU CAN ABOUT YOUR PRODUCT.

KNOW YOUR TERRITORY

EACH SALESMAN MUST WATCH THE DEVELOPMENTS AND CHANGES THAT ARE TAKING PLACE IN HIS OWN TERRITORY, AND BE QUICK TO COVER THE NEWCOMERS IN THE AREA. THE MORE NIMBLE YOU ARE IN WATCHING DEVELOPMENTS, THE BETTER JUMP YOU GET ON YOUR COMPETITORS. RE-EXAMINE YOUR ROUTINE FOR COVERING YOUR TERRITORY. IF YOU HAVE NOT CHANGED IT IN ANY WAY FOR THE PAST FEW YEARS, THERE IS ONLY ONE POSSIBLE CONCLUSION: YOUR GEOGRAPHIC AREA HAS STOOD STILL WHILE MOST OF THE COUNTRY HAS BEEN DOING SOMERSAULTS...

LEARNING FROM LOSS

THERE NEVER WAS A 100% PERFECT SALESMAN WHO CLOSED EVERY SALE, ON EVERY CALL - AND THERE NEVER WILL BE. BUT YOU CAN STEADILY INCREASE YOUR "BATTING AVERAGE" IF, WHEN YOU LOSE A SALE, YOU ASK YOURSELF HONESTLY , "WHAT DID I DO, OR FAIL TO DO, WHICH CAUSED THAT SALE TO

SLIP THROUGH MY FINGERS?" "WHAT CAN I DO TO AVOID THE SAME THING AGAIN?"

IN BRIEF: A PHILOSOPHY OF SALESMANSHIP THE WRITINGS OF S.L. HEINE, SR. CONSIST OF MANY SHORT ITEMS THAT PRESENT A CAPSULE VIEW OF HIS IDEAS ABOUT SELLING. HERE ARE SOME EXAMPLES:

BE A REAL SALESMAN:

THE NEW YOUNG SALESMAN ASKED HIS SALES MANAGER IF HE COULD REFUND THE MONEY TO AN IRATE CUSTOMER WHO DISCOVERED THAT THE LOT HE HAD BOUGHT WAS UNDER WATER."WHAT KIND OF A SALESMAN ARE YOU" DEMANDED THE SALES MANAGER. "GO OUT THERE AND SELL HIM A MOTOR BOAT."

"THANK YOU:"

THANK YOU FOR SENDING BUSINESS OUR WAY. THERE'S NOTHING WE LIKE TO DO MORE THAN SAY "THANKS" TO YOU - OUR CUSTOMER. WE HOPE YOU NEVER FIND US GUILTY OF FAILING TO EXPRESS OUR APPRECIATION FOR YOUR ORDERS. WE KNOW THAT YOU ARE RESPONSIBLE FOR KEEPING US IN BUSINESS.

KNOW YOURSELF:

THERE IS NO SUBSTITUTE FOR THE HEALTHY PROCESS OF INTROSPECTION AND SELF-ANALYSIS. LEADERSHIP CAN BE ELUSIVE UNTIL YOU CAN REASONABLY, THOROUGHLY

AND COLDLY EVALUATE YOUR ASSETS AND YOUR LIABILITIES AS A PREAMBLE TO SELF-IMPROVEMENT.

ENTHUSIASM CAN KEEP YOU GOING:

A TOP SALESMAN HAS WHAT I CALL EMOTIONAL STAMINA PLUS ENTHUSIASM. HE HAS WHAT MANY SPORTS WRITERS REFER TO AS "HEART ." THE COURAGE AND STAMINA TO KEEP GOING WHEN THE GOING GETS TOUGHER! THE DETERMINATION TO FIGHT EVEN HARDER WHEN DEFEAT SEEMS SO NEAR! ARE YOU THAT KIND OF SALESMAN?

I HOPE YOU ARE NOT IN THIS CATEGORY:

WHEN A MAN WROTE TO THE B.F. GOODRICH COMPANY ASKING FOR SOME INFORMATION, HE ADDED, "I DON'T WANT ANY ADVERTISING MATERIAL - AND NO SALESMEN. "

IT WAS DIFFICUL T TO PUT THE INFORMATION INTO A LETTER, SO THE COMPANY IGNORED THE WARNING AND SENT A SALESMAN.THE FELLOW DIDN'T WAIT FOR AN EXPLANATION.

"I TOLD THEM," HE SAID TO THE SALESMAN, "NO SALESMEN!"

THE CALLER - A YOUNGSTER JUST OUT OF THE COMPANY'S TRAINING SCHOOL- SIGHED AND REPLIED, "MISTER, I'M AS CLOSE TO A NO-SALESMAN AS THEY'VE GOT. "

"Mr. Heine"

Retirement!
Sam and "Mr. Heine"

JANUARY 1st

A NEW YEAR'S PRAYER, PART 4

The unselfish spirit of human brotherhood -- which has been taught us through the centuries as the only ideal that makes any sense -- may yet produce a moral force greater than battleships and planes, tanks, guns and the atomic bomb.

But such a force cannot be mobilized unless every one of us in our contacts with other human beings from day to day learns the lesson of sacrifice and selflessness...

JANUARY 2nd

A NEW YEAR'S PRAYER, PART 5

Almighty God, give us understanding so that we may begin to live in accordance with thy wishes -- so they we may begin to mobilize our nation and all other nations in the greatest spiritual crusade of all time.

We shall, to be sure, promise and we may perhaps falter. We shall pledge our faith but we may sin. We shall stumble, but we will move on toward that triumph of soul, which the human race seeks under thy guidance -- the victory over pride and ego, the victory over greed and intolerance.

We know that in war itself there can be no victory -- only in peace that comes from forgiveness and understanding.

JANUARY 3rd

ONE DAY A MONTH

Your future in selling is in your hands.

If you will devote one day a month to develop yourself, your product knowledge and your general selling skills, you will be amazed at the overall improvement in these areas in less than a year.

Believe me, it is worth the effort.

You are capable of being an even better salesman than you are.

JANUARY 4th

LIVE UNTIL YOU DIE

I received this sound advice many years ago from a lawyer friend who had an arrested case of tuberculosis.

This friend knew he would have to live a regulated life, but this hasn't stopped him from practicing law, rearing a fine family and really enjoying life. My friend, who is now 78 years old, expresses his philosophy in these words:

"I'm going to live until I die, and I'm not going to get life and death confused. While I'm on this earth, I'm going to live. Why be only half alive?"

Every minute a person spends worrying about dying is just one minute that fellow might as well have been dead.

JANUARY 5th

BIBLE LESSON

There is not a lesson taught or a doctrine given in the New or Old Testament that does not strengthen the qualities of salesmanship.

Faith and religion imbue a person with the basic character qualities such as stability, courage and self-discipline.

Often I hesitate to offer such advice, for fear of being thought of as a preacher.

But such advice is without a doubt both practical and rewarding to those who might want to follow it.

JANUARY 6th

KNOW YOUR TERRITORY

Each salesman must watch the developments and changes that are taking place in his own territory, and be quick to cover the newcomers in the area.

The more nimble you are in watching developments, the better jump you get on your competitors.

Re-examine your routine for covering your territory. Make it a point on your very next trip to compare the territory with what it was when you first took it on.

That will give you the clues to the sales opportunities you might have missed, and will tell you if you've been losing ground by following the old routine year in and year out.

JANUARY 7th

LESS IS MORE

A creative salesman does not worry about losing business volume when his territory is cut.

He looks upon it as a compliment and a challenge to make bigger buyers of his present customers, and to find new profitable accounts among the prospects he previously had no time to develop.

A sales manager usually has a good reason behind his decision to reduce a salesman's territory.

In most cases he knows that there is more business in the old territory that any one man can possibly get.

JANUARY 8th

THE VALUE OF SERVICE

You can increase your share of a customer's business by thinking up a better service for him.

Especially, offer him something extra -- some convenience he will appreciate; some personal attention that will prove your interest in his business; some suggestion that proves your alertness to his needs.

This is one way that you, as a creative salesman, can gain a customer's increasing dependence on you as a main supplier.

JANUARY 9th
CREATIVE SELLING

Today more than ever before, business executives are looking for creativeness in the men they hire.

This is because our times demand originality.

"The man of the hour is not the man who is the strongest, craftiest, shrewdest or most popular. He is the man of exceptional originality. He is the man who has disciplined himself to keep acquiring new knowledge and skills."

The same remark goes for salesmen.

JANUARY 10th
CREATIVE SELLING, PART 2

Typical of the stress on creativeness is this statement from one company's bid for salesmen:

"Today's salesmen must know not only his company's policies, products and methods; but he must also be able to correlate them with present and future market potentials and trends.

"Thus, to succeed, he must be creative in his activities in order to expand markets and increase the use of his products.

"The creative salesman who measures up to the challenge before him has unlimited avenues for advancement and for increased income."

JANUARY 11th

CREATIVE SELLING PART, Part 3

Any salesman or supervisor can pick up orders, check stocks, answer phone or mail inquiries and add high mileage on his car.

These are necessary activities in selling, but they are not creative.

Creative salesmen earn big money because they bring their imagination and ideas into play in every step of the selling process.

If you are going to make money, you have to know how to create a demand for what you sell.

This is the heart of selling. It takes imagination, it takes ideas, but it pays off.

JANUARY 12th
CREATIVE SELLING, PART, Part 4

Have you ever found a prospect in cold canvassing?

Have you ever gotten an appointment with a prospect who was hard to see?

Have you ever created a desire for your product or service in a prospect who was not much interested when you started your interview?

If you can answer "Yes" to any of these questions, you have proved that you can be creative.

Now the question is, have you been creative enough

JANUARY 13th
CREATIVE SELLING, PART 5

Everyone has imagination. With it you dream, visualize, invent or create.

Imagination lends a magical touch to features and talking points of a product or service.

With imagination, the talking points set the fire of desire.

The power of imagination makes it possible for you to help your customers visualize the profit in your company's line, the value in your merchandise and the desirability of your cooperation.

JANUARY 14th

CREATIVE SELLING, PART 6

A salesman who is imaginative is also curious.

He is eager to obtain knowledge, to find out the "how," "when," "where" and "what" of everything that pertains to his job.

Curiosity becomes a habit with him.

Without curiosity a salesman cannot expect to achieve any real measure of success. Without curiosity we cannot open new avenues for the sale of our products.

We remain only a parasite living upon the results obtained through the curiosity of an inquisitive predecessor.

JANUARY 15th

CREATIVE SELLING, PART 7

Imagination resides in the salesman who sits down quietly every evening and thinks of the things that happened during the day, trying to think up better ways to handle the situations that didn't work out well.

It resides to a greater extend in the salesman who spends an hour at home each night thinking abut his customers and their problems, letting his mind run riot on ways to solve their problems and built up their business so that he can sell more to them.

JANUARY 16th

CREATIVE SELLING, PART 8

Regardless of what your job may be, you can acquire imagination by this simple practice:

Imagine yourself handling your job like a star salesman.

Dissect your job piece by piece, and imagine all the things you would do in difficult situations.

Write down your ideas so you don't forget them.

Don't be afraid of wild ideas -- they frequently straighten themselves out when you think them through, and you can often adapt them in your job.

JANUARY 17th

A MATTER OF FAITH

The more you know about your product, the stronger your faith in its performance.

The more faith, the most conviction you have in selling.

You may feel that you already know all you have to about that you are selling, but you must remember that it is the salesman who know the MOST who reaches the top.

JANUARY 18th

PRODUCT KNOWLEDGE

Write down all the points about the product that you can think of from memory. Scrape your mind for every single feature that might be a selling feature, including ones that you are aware of but aren't using now in your presentation.

Review carefully all company literature and bulletins for points that you have forgotten or overlooked.

In most cases you can and should enlarge the company list from your own knowledge of the product and its use.

JANUARY 19th

WHY THEY BUY

Your presentation must satisfy the prospect's buying motives.

Buying motives are satisfied not by lists of impressive features, but by the benefits that those features will give. There is a clear distinction between the two.

A person does not buy strength; he buys the durability that strength provides.

He does not buy beauty; he buys the pleasure and pride that possession of a beautiful object will mean.

He does not buy speed; he buys the time saving, or the greater production, or the excitement that speed gives him.

Behind everything the prospect wants, there is the more important reason why he wants it.

JANUARY 20th

IN HIS SHOES

To select your most telling sales features, put yourself in the prospect's place.

Look carefully at every point and ask, "Is that what would satisfy my buying motives if I were the prospect?"

Remember that he is the judge and that he will buy only what promises to do something for HIM.

Remember also that the better you know your competition, the better you can select and utilize the features that are yours alone.

JANUARY 21st

SEEING IS BELIEVING

The best way to convey to a prospect the benefits he'll gain by buying your product is by a visual demonstration.

A visual demonstration tells your prospect more than you can explain in twice the time by words alone, and much more clearly.

This is because seeing is the most important of the fine senses for comprehension.

JANUARY 22nd

KNOW YOUR WEAKNESSES

Where is your selling weakest?

Do you find people difficult? Are you too lazy to give time to studying techniques? Are you inclined to be indifferent to problems, and likely to take the easiest way out in any given situation? Are you easily overcome by a defeatist attitude?

I don't know of any more brutal experience in any man's life than facing and answering these questions honestly to himself.

But you should take a frank and healthy look at yourself to determine where your greatest weakness lies:

AND DETERMINE TO DO SOMETHING ABOUT IT.

JANUARY 23rd

LIVING WITH FAILURE

When we really accept ourselves we realize that failure is a part of life.

When a failure comes it isn't traumatic. The basic decision in regard to it has already been made, thus we are free to respond to the conditions brought by failure with deliberate decision rather than despair.

This is the only way we can grow. Never to enter unexplored territory where we may get lost, never to engage ourselves in a task that may end in failure -- this is the way to stagnation and death.

To launch out into the unknown, to attempt the untried and the uncertain -- this is the way to vitality and life.

JANUARY 24th

SPEAKING OF SALES

Those who shy away from a "canned sales talk" should do so -- if the talk is written as one would write it, rather than as one should say it.

Often, a well-written sentence can be reconstructed to use in spoken form, by shifting the position of verbs, etc., to make it more effective.

It takes some people longer than others to master good speech.

None of us ever master completely the basic elements and principles of speaking and writing, but if we are aware of them and if we continue to study them, our competence is bound to increase.

JANUARY 25th

DON'T DROP OUT

One just can't "drop out" of school and "drop into" sales work and be a good representative for his company and its product.

Drop-outs, whether from high school or college, have three strikes against them: they haven't completed the job they set out to do (graduate), a high percentage of them aren't as dependable as salesman have to be, and they haven't mastered spoken and written English.

The lack of effective communications hinders advancement in all areas of work above that of manual labor, and is glaringly conspicuous in salesmanship.

JANUARY 26th

NOT "GOOD ENOUGH"

Unfortunately, the attitude of many people toward their work is "I guess that's good enough," "That'll do," "What difference does it make?" and "What's it to me?"

They fail to realize that "good enough" is not enough.

Only our best will pass the test in today's highly competitive economy. The people who get ahead, and the companies that get ahead, are those who strive for excellence.

JANUARY 27th
CREAM OF THE CROP

As cream rises to the top of a bottle of milk, the real value of an employee always rises to the top and is recognized.

Every job is like a savings account. The more you put into it, the more valuable you make it, and more you get out of it.

We must give more to our jobs before we can get more out of them.

If your attitude toward your job is "What do I get out of it?" rather than "What can I put into it?" don't wonder why you are by-passed when promotions are handed out.

JANUARY 28th
WHY WAIT?

There are two kinds of people in the world: the waiters and the doers.

The waiter thinks about how things could be better.

The doer WORKS to make them better.

Good intentions count for nothing unless you take the necessary action to convert your desires into reality.

When did you last say, "I meant to do that" about reading some literature regarding our product line, calling a friend, writing a letter, or whatever? If you are like most of us, your answer is probably "more often than I like to think about."

JANUARY 29th

KEEP MOVING

Business is like riding a bicycle: either you keep moving or you fall down. To stand still is to be run over.

You've got to be willing to fight your way to the top, or you'll never get there.

Any man who wants to make a success in the business world today needs nerve, courage, rugged tenacity, tough-mindedness -- and plenty of each!

You've got to pursue success with bulldog determination, seize your opportunity when it knocks, and even blow your own horn if necessary. This isn't cynicism, it's realism, and you know it.

JANUARY 30th

READING FOR SUCCESS

Read inspirational books of great leaders in government and business.

They will give the reader some insight into what greatness really is: A belief, fundamentally, in something greater than one's own self.

It is religious in nature, though not necessarily sectarian; it pervades and sweeps through a man's life like a tidal wave, carrying everything with it. In discovering the main characteristics of most top executives, the conclusion has been reached that nearly all have a basic, religious motivation.

This would indicate, then, that salesmen could borrow a page from their book by adapting some of the same beliefs, as fuel for their lives.

JANUARY 31st

KEEP YOUR DIGNITY

Don't debase yourself by "souping around" your superiors.

Everyone likes personal service, likes to have someone fawn over him, run errands, wait on his every wish (even the boss is human), but don't YOU be the "soup."

Be social, be cooperative, be self-confident enough to know that you're something bigger than a messenger boy,

Never beg. Never tattle on fellow salesmen or employees. It will hurt you in your own eyes!

FEBRUARY 1st

A FRESH VIEW

Change your point of view for a day to open your eyes and see yourself and your behavior in a new light.

Act as if it was your last day on the job; look around you as if you would never see your surroundings again.

Look at the people around you and try to figure out how they regard you: Do they think you are timid, or courageous, or persuasive?

You may never come up with the answers, but the effort will teach you many things about yourself.

FEBRUARY 2nd

KEEP RECORDS

How many of you know from one week to the next how your sales compare with the same period last year?

Do you keep a tally sheet of your sales?

How many of you have enough interest in your job to keep a record of your sales?

Do you keep a route book showing where you go each day?

Record-keeping may seem tedious and necessary, but it tells you how you are doing at present, how you did in the past, and can give you a goal to shoot for in the future.

FEBRUARY 3rd

LOOK IN THE MIRROR

Practice your sales presentation by giving it OUT LOUD in front of a mirror, using the mirror as a prospect. Try as hard as you can to turn that mirror from a prospect into a customer.

Look hard at yourself while you're making your presentation. What does the prospect see? An alert, concerned, well-groomed, confident salesman? Someone who can give him service after the sale?

If the answer is no, or you're not sure, try again. A self-appraisal can open your eyes to facts you can learn in no other way.

FEBRUARY 4th

A VITAL ROLE

Cultivate the habit of thinking of your job as the part of the operation that brings in the money; that makes all of the other jobs possible, and produces the profit that keeps the company in business.

Do that and you will find in your job a more thrilling challenge, that will help you make more sales, more customers and more profit for your company both in good times and "not so good" times as well.

Remember, we sell -- or we sink.

FEBRUARY 5th

YOU AND YOUR COMPANY

Some employees feel that their pay checks are their due, whether they do anything to earn them or not, and they it's smart to get away with anything they can.

They want still more money, still more time off, more leisure, more vacations, more sick leave, more retirement pay, but would be insulted if they were asked to produce more in order to earn these things.

If management is to be concerned with the well-being of its employees, it is certainly only fair that employees be concerned with the well-being of the company they're expecting to pay their rent, buy their clothes and food and send their kids to school.

FEBRUARY 6th

THE VALUE OF RECOGNITION

Dedicated employees are something every business needs almost as much as customers.

They're like a magnet that draws in more customers.

But today management seems to be getting away from complimenting people on a job well done, or rewarding them for a good suggestion.

Too often management is inclined to accept suggestions as its due and then claim credit for them itself.

Nothing kills employee initiative quicker. Recognition, plus a suitable raise, is the quickest way to create a dedicated employee.

FEBRUARY 7th

VICES AND VIRTUES

Recently I reviewed my own sales record with a critical eye. I checked into some of my selling vices and virtues.

First, I discovered business was good with customers where I had gained their complete confidence.

Second, business was spotty with those I had not taken time or thought to pull closer to me.

Third, in almost every instance my scribbled records disclosed the planned days better than the haphazard ones.

The sound principles of long-range selling remain unchanged over the years.

FEBRUARY 8th

PRACTICE, PRACTICE, PRACTICE

Those who shy away from selling as a career do not understand that the recruit salesman can no more expect to go out and write a great volume of business the first day in the field than a lawyer could expect to dash from his graduation exercises to the courtroom and match his wits with an experienced opposing counsel and hope to sway the jury with his appeal.

It takes practice -- thoughtful practice, constant practice.

FEBRUARY 9th

A FUNDAMENTAL IDEA

Let me suggest that you get the following idea firmly planted in your mind, because it is fundamental -- you just can't escape it:

"Business profits do not come from making things, but from selling the things that business makes."

Turn that idea over in your mind -- slowly -- because you must understand and believe it in order to succeed; in order to survive

FEBRUARY 10th

TOUGH TIMES MAKE US TOUGH

Here's something I know to be a fact: The best salesmen and most enduring businesses emerge from the tough competitive periods, not from those easy-going, "order-taking" periods when orders fairly "grown on trees" and all you need to make a sale is an order book and a smile.

Why, some of the most successful businesses in America actually STARTED in periods of depression.

I know one that started in 1930 with very few tangible assets, but with a handful of fighting salesmen who knew that if they didn't sell they didn't eat

The company survived and prospered.

"Guts" did it.

FEBRUARY 11th

INTEGRITY IS VITAL

The importance of integrity cannot be overlooked in analyzing the basis of lasting, constructive sales leadership.

We are not thinking here of the sales leader being a paragon of virtue, but as being basically honest with himself and honest with other people -- his customers and prospects, his associates, his superiors, even his competitors.

The sales leader must have a well-developed sense of responsibility and a solid reputation for keeping his word.

You cannot look up to a man you do not fully trust.

FEBRUARY 12th

CONFIDENCE, ENTHUSIASM

A salesman needs both confidence and enthusiasm, and sometimes confidence wins out over enthusiasm.

For example, a salesman might not be enthusiastic about facing an angry customer, but he can be confident he can handle the situation and soothe the customer's ruffled feelings

Just as you couldn't say Eisenhower was enthusiastic over the invasion of Europe, but he was confident it would succeed.

FEBRUARY 13th

HISTORY LESSON

Do you want to become enthusiastic about your industry? Read its history.

In order to be enthusiastic about one's work, one must visualize what that work is doing for the benefit of mankind.

All growing companies seek to advance one type of man -- he who develops superior knowledge regarding the work he is doing. In short, the salesman who does not genuinely want to perform his duty in the most efficient manner is a liability to any company. The sooner he is replaced by an enthusiastic, sincere salesman, the better it is for all concerned, including himself.

FEBRUARY 14th

DON'T KNOCK THE BOSS

To the salesman on the road comes the temptation to take sides with his customers against the house that employs him. This destroys the buyer's confidence in the salesman's firm.

Do not appear to be disloyal to your company in your efforts to be accommodating to your customer.

I like to meet the man who is glad he is working for the "old man." That man does more than printed advertising can ever do. His loyalty inspired the buyer's confidence in the firm he represents.

Smiley Anders

FEBRUARY 15th

YOU AND YOUR COMPETITORS

In former times competitors were sworn enemies and could say no good word about the other, but recently they have been more inclined to adopt an attitude of neutrality, if not one of open friendship.

The reasons are not difficult to discover. People have been learning to live in contact with their fellows as populations grew more dense. These are not pioneer days, when men lived isolated lives.

But competitors and competing goods can best be placed in the background by describing thoroughly the merit of the goods you are trying to sell.

To sell goods on their merits, rather than on the demerits of competitors' goods, is good salesmanship.

FEBRUARY 16th

DO YOU LIKE PEOPLE?

A genuine liking for people is an invaluable trait for the successful salesman who has a sincere interest in the behavior of human beings, their attitudes, interests, personalities and personal problems.

To get along well with people, salesmen must be tolerant and patient with their likes and dislikes.

Salesmen just be genuinely interested in helping others to solve their personal problems and secure greater satisfaction from life.

FEBRUARY 17th

HANDLING OBJECTIONS

"I have no calls for your product," says the customer.

The successful salesman answers, "I'm not at all surprised.

Do you ever have any calls for a haircut or a shave? Of course not. But you would if you displayed a red-and-white barber's pole. It is the same with our product. All you have to do is display it in a conspicuous place, and I will surely sell you more on my next trip.

"Our product will sell just as soon as people see you carry it in stock. If they didn't buy it, we couldn't have stayed in business so long, could we?"

FEBRUARY 18th

MAN'S SIX MISTAKES

By Cicero:

1. The delusion that individual advancement is made by crushing others.

2. The tendency to worry about things that cannot be changed or corrected.

3. Insisting that a thing is impossible because we cannot accomplish it.

4. Refusing to set aside trivial preferences.

5. Neglecting development and refinement of the mind, and not acquiring the habit of reading and study.

6. Attempting to compel other persons to believe and live as we do.

FEBRUARY 19th

FIGHTING FEAR

Young salesman must conquer fear of failure, fear of embarrassment, fear of meeting a belligerent prospect, fear of indefinable things.

Some old-timers in the selling business will confess that they, too, have a momentary period of "torture" just before they are to face up to a new prospect.

But they have learned how to bridle nervousness, to convert this energy into energy for the job to be done, and into a sale.

Your knowledge of your product or service makes you a specialist on the subject. You know more about it than the prospect does, and this should make you sure of yourself.

FEBRUARY 20th

BEN'S PHILOSOPHY

Benjamin Franklin's autobiography contains some rules and resolutions that may prove helpful in these difficult and uncertain times:

1. It is necessary for me to be extremely frugal till I have paid what I owe.

2. To endeavor to speak truth in every instance; to give nobody expectations that are not likely to be answered, but aim at sincerity in every word and action...

3. To apply myself industriously to whatever business I take in hand, and not divert my mind from my business by any foolish project of growing suddenly rich; for industry and patience are the surest measures of plenty.

4. I resolve to speak ill of no man whatever, not even in a matter of truth; but rather by some means excuse the faults I hear charged upon others, and upon proper occasions speak all the good I know of everybody.

FEBRUARY 21st

POISONOUS THINKING

You may be polite and courteous to someone in your office, but when his back is turned, you are very critical and resentful toward him in your mind.

Such negative thoughts are highly destructive to you. It is like taking poison.You are actually taking mental poisons which rob you of vitality, enthusiasm, strength, guidance and good will.

These negative thoughts and emotions sink down into your subconscious, and cause all kinds of difficulties and maladies in your life.

"Judge not, that ye be not judged..."

FEBRUARY 22nd

TO THE CUSTOMER

It is our sincere wish that the first sip of Morning Treat coffee you have in the morning is a testimony to the quality of our product.

We are not the largest coffee company in America -- or even in Louisiana -- but we take a personal interest in each package that leaves our plant.

We are still old-fashioned enough to believe that every package of coffee represents each of us personally and is not simply the product of a corporate symbol.

We have had 60 years of experience doing one job exceptionally well...roasting quality coffee.

We would be happy to have you take a sip of our quality.

FEBRUARY 23rd

TO THE SALES FORCE:

Statistics prove that more businesses fail from the sin of complacency than any other reason...

Your company HAS NOT, and WILL NOT, cloak itself in the shroud of complacency.

And we will positively not allow our employees to do so.

Unless you are determined to put forth an all-out effort in order to increase your sales, and rid yourself of the taint of complacency, I suggest you seek other employment.

FEBRUARY 24th

THE LOYALTY TEST

Ask yourself these questions to test your loyalty to the company:

1. Do you work just as efficiently and conscientiously when the boss is away?

2. If you happened to overheard critical comments about the company, would you voluntarily take the company's side?

3. Would you willingly do more than you are paid to do, if it were of value to the company?

4. Do you honestly feel that it is partly your responsibility to be continuously mindful of the importance and value of the customer's satisfaction?

5. Even if it meant missing a personal appointment, or giving up some of your own time, would you gladly put the company's interests ahead of your own?

FEBRUARY 25th

THE LOYALTY TEST, PART 2

6. Do you carefully check everything you do, and everything that clears through you, in order to be sure that it meets the company's requirements and standards?

7. Do you regularly make suggestions which you feel may be of value to the company?

8. Do you agree, wholeheartedly, with the principle that only your best is good enough and you owe it to your company to give your best, always?

9. Do you try to maintain a pleasant, cooperative attitude toward your fellow workers, at all levels?

10. Do you feel that it is partly your responsibility to assist new employees to become adjusted, and to help them to become valuable employees of the company?

FEBRUARY 26th

THE LOYALTY TEST, PART 3

11. Do you feel that you are a part of the company, that whatever your job happens to be it is important and that your future with the company is up to you?

12. Do you do all that you possibly can to avoid being absent from work; and do you do your best to discourage absenteeism on the part of fellow workers?

13. Do you devote a part of your spare time to reading and studying that will help you to become of more value to the company?

14. Do you take a personal interest in helping the company to avoid unnecessary waste of time, money and materials?

15. Do you willingly do things which need to be done without waiting to be told to do them?

FEBRUARY 27th

THE LOYALTY TEST, PART 4

16. Do you agree with the old saying that "A man who never does more than he's paid for is never paid more for what he does?"

17. Do you feel that no business can be any better than the men and women who work for it?

18. Do you have a feeling of genuine pride in your company, so that you take a personal interest in its progress?

19. Do you consider yourself a member of a team of men and women, all working for one common cause?

20. Do you agree with the statement that "Nothing can take the place of loyalty in any job?"

FEBRUARY 28th

FIND THE CUSTOMER

The recipe for rabbit pie in an old English cookbook starts out "First, catch the rabbit."

The recipe for salesmanship has just as plain a first step: "First, find a customer."

The only way to catch a rabbit is to get out into the field. The only way to find a customer is to get out and make calls, than make more calls.

See the people!

FEBRUARY 29th (when needed)

SKILL AND WORK

Skill is not a substitute for work. Skill is applying proven techniques to work.

A lot of work done efficiently produces maximum results. Sales are first made in the mind of a salesman, or they are never made at all.

Expect to make sales, but do not expect them to make themselves

MARCH 1st

SALESMEN: THE BAD AND THE GOOD

<u>The Bad</u>

When a man wrote to the B.F. Goodrich Company asking for some information, he added, "I don't want any advertising material -- and no salesman."

It was difficult to put the information into a letter, so the company ignored the warning and sent a salesman. The fellow didn't wait for an explanation: "I told them," he said to the salesman, "No salesman!"

The caller -- a youngster just out of the company's training school -- sighed and replied, "Mister, I'm as close to a no-salesman as they've got."

<u>The Good</u>

The new young salesman asked his sales manager if he could refund the money to an irate customer who discovered that the lot he had bought was under water.

"What kind of a salesman are you?" demanded the sales manager. "Go out there and sell him a motor boat."

MARCH 2nd

ENTHUSIASM CAN KEEP YOU GOING

A top salesman has what I call emotional stamina, plus enthusiasm.

He has what many sports writers refer to as "heart" -- the courage and stamina to keep going when the going gets tougher. It's the determination to fight even harder when defeat seems near.

It's the kind of guts that makes if possible for a baseball team losing by 5 or 6 runs going into the last inning to play so hard and so well that they come out of the inning as winners.

It's the kind of determination that makes it possible for a champion fighter to get up off the floor after he's been knocked down, and to spring back into the fight with such fury that he comes out a winner. This is the kind of stamina and "bounce-back" that all champion salesmen have -- an ability to keep going in the face of frustrations, turndowns and defeats.

Are you that kind of salesman?

MARCH 3rd

KNOW YOURSELF

Benjamin Franklin was no match for some of the brilliant statesmen of his day in oratory or a few other special attributes.

However, his versatility -- the balance of his leadership qualities -- put him high in the hall of fame.

Incidentally, Franklin made a statement that seems appropriate here: "Every man I meet is in some way my superior. And in that I learn from him."

Usually the process of self-evaluation will suggest to the salesman some logical steps he can take to improve his own leadership capabilities. The desire to achieve is capable of being controlled and developed.

MARCH 4th

BOSS VS. LEADER

A boss creates fear; a leader creates confidence.

A boss creates resentment; a leader creates enthusiasm.

A boss fixes blame; a leader fixes mistakes.

A boss knows how; a leader shows how.

A boss can make work drudgery; a leader can make it interesting.

A boss relies on authority; a leader relies on cooperation.

A boss drives; a leader leads.

A boss can become a leader -- but not overnight. He must first adjust his attitude about people in general and his subordinates in particular.

He must develop the personal touch -- let the employee know where he stands; discuss progress, listen to his ideas; inform him in advance of changes; let him know you want to help him.

And remember this: "Do as you would have your workers do."

MARCH 5th
IGNORANCE AND STUPIDITY

Do you know the difference between ignorance and stupidity? If you don't know the difference, you're ignorant.

If you still don't know the difference after I've explained the difference, you're stupid.

Ignorance is nothing more than the lack of information. I'm ignorant when it comes to, say, laying bricks.

It's no shame to be ignorant. We're all ignorant of far more things in the world than we can ever know. But it is a shame to be ignorant in the field in which we spent the majority of our time, the field upon which we depend for a livelihood.

If I could be permitted only one thing to say to a young man or woman, I would way this: "Choose carefully a line of endeavor to which you will dedicate your life. Then each day spend some time reducing your ignorance in that line. Sooner or later, if you'll stay with it, you will find yourself at or near the top of the field you've selected."

MARCH 6th

THE MAN WITH ONE ARM

A good friend of mine came home from Europe in 1945 minus one arm. Despite his handicap, John is always smiling, always helping others. He's about as optimistic as anyone I know.

"It's just an arm," he said. "Sure, two are better than one. But my spirit is 100 percent intact. I'm really grateful for that."

Another amputee friend is an excellent golfer. One day I asked him how he had been able to develop such a near-perfect style.

"Well," he said, "it's my experience that the right attitude and one arm will beat the wrong attitude and two arms every time."

Think about that for a while...

MARCH 7th

WORDS ARE GOLDEN

"The worst enemy of communications is the illusion of it."

How true this is in the field of selling! Salesmen make hundreds of calls every year, using hundreds of thousands of words, but frequently no real communication takes place.

Thousands of sales are lost not only because we talk too much, but also because we don't think through what we really want to say. Samson was a piker; he killed a thousand men with the jawbone of an ass. Every hour in the day ten thousand sales are killed with the same weapon.

It is my conviction that one of the most important features of a salesman's responsibility is to improve himself in effective speaking. Listen to a recording of your own voice -- see how you can improve it. This could pay big dividends.

MARCH 8th

THE FIVE QUESTIONS

Ask yourself these five questions at least once a month:

1. Have I been working every day without a definite and specific goal?

2. Am I accepting customer refusal on the first suggestion as final?

3. Have I succumbed to "law of average" thinking?

4. Have I been probing every prospect and customer for leads to additional sales?

5. Have I become so eager for big sales that I have neglected the small ones?

These questions could form the basis of a nightly one-minute checkup by every salesman who refuses to be satisfied with the business he is doing today.

MARCH 9th

THE IMPORTANCE OF SERVICE

Have you ever thought of what would happen if garbage wasn't collected?

Or if drug stores weren't kept open on Sundays and evenings?

Or if some filling stations didn't stay open all night?

Or if proprietors of delicatessens went home early?

Or if buses didn't run at night?

These are humble services performed by inconspicuous people. But the people who clean the streets and buildings while we sleep are a vital cog in the machinery of daily life.

The person who does his job as well as he possibly can and is dependable -- this person is important.

Whoever finds contentment in his work and is needed is a success.

MARCH 10th

LOVE STORY

All the opportunities in the world are waiting to be grasped by people who are in love with what they're doing.

Nothing great was ever achieved without enthusiasm.

Enthusiasm is the major quality of every professional salesman. It overcomes inertia, banishes discouragement, gets things done -- and the remarkable thing about it is that it's contagious.

Enthusiasm is the state of caring -- really caring -- about something.

Always look for it in others -- when you find it, strike sparks from it.

Some of those sparks will kindle a fire in YOU!

Love life -- and your work.

Believe me, it will love you right back.

MARCH 11th

A MATTER OF PRIORITIES

A glaring failure of our modern world is that it has taught us how to get and have -- and neglected to teach us how to live.

Training in character has failed to keep pace with science and technology. We are technical giants, but moral and spiritual adolescents. God intended man to have things, but He wanted man to possess his possessions, not to BE possessed by them. Possessions were to be man's tools, not his master.

Man was made to love people and use things. So often he loves things and uses people.

MARCH 12th

SELF RESPECT

What one word best sums up the meaning of life to you? My answer is "self respect."

The fun and challenge of living is to meet a standard of excellence.

Work your problems out for yourself; you have to learn to live without crying on someone else's shoulder. A measure of a person is how he can hurdle the problems of existence on his own, and without self-pity.

If you turn this over to someone else and say, "Handle this for me," you're defaulting on the whole idea of living. Meet and face your responsibilities; don't expect someone else to do this for you.

MARCH 13th

BE SINCERE

There are few things so empty as the perfunctory "Good morning,"

The disinterested "How are you?" or the thousand other phrases meaninglessly uttered out of mechanical politeness.

They are like songs with no melody; just hollow, carelessly recited lyrics. A hundred of them are not worth the one spontaneous "Glad to meet you," accompanied by the music of sincerity.

MARCH 14th

THE POWER OF PRAISE

In a study conducted by Western Reserve University, recognition was found to be one of the most significant factors contributing to the motivation of professional personnel. It was more important than responsibility, salary, advancement or the work itself.

In spite of its importance, the ability to give praise or credit is lacking in many managers.

Recognition is vital because it not only gives the individual a feeling that his efforts are appreciated, but affords him a benchmark as to his progress.

MARCH 15th

THE LOST CUSTOMERS

Public relations, the art of making friends, is important in your business. One recent survey revealed that the following losses of customers are typical:

1% are lost through death;

3% are lost by moving to another area;

9% leave to buy at lower prices;

14% leave because of unadjusted complaints;

68% leave because of indifference and lack of interest.

It's surprising what a warm smile and greeting will do.

MARCH 16th

WHAT'S A "NATURAL-BORN SALESMAN?"

When anyone says a man is a natural-born salesman, he is perpetuating a myth. The designation implies that the ability to sell is primarily a native one; that the person is a spell-binder.

Actually, any normal person interested in selling can learn, and having learned, can practice selling successfully.

The spell-binder who cannot answer technical questions is quite likely to lose the order to a competing salesman who may have a less glib tongue but can demonstrate the worth and application of his product.

Popularity and friendship are genuine assets in salesmanship. But the day is gone, if it ever really existed, when the salesman who got to the top was the one who did the best job of selling himself.

MARCH 17th

THE VALUE OF EDUCATION

Before he can educate his prospect, the salesman must educate himself. Salesmanship has become a profession. It has become more of a science than an art.

The education of the active salesman must take place largely through reading, study and observation. He must get the facts about his company's history, development, growth, management, reputation and place in the industry. He must know all about the products he has to sell. He must also know the specific types of competition he will meet in the field.

At some point you will be brought up short if you continue year in and year out to tell the same sales story, use the same approaches and the same presentation. Stay aware of the continuing need for change.

Life itself is a continuing process in which imperceptible changes are always taking place. They become discernible when we stop to examine the present and make comparisons with the past.

Since selling is, in a sense, a catering to human needs, it changes gradually as our customs and behavior change. You must stop now and then to get your selling methods into focus with the times.

MARCH 18th

A LIFE'S WORK

Can you definitely say, "I have made up my mind to be a good salesman?

Salesmanship is a life's work. It has its own body of knowledge and information, its own techniques, and its own skills. It demands the same firmness of purpose to assure success as medicine or any other calling. Nobody should choose it for his profession who would be happier doing something else, or who is not prepared to put into it everything he has.

Take a few minutes and have a heart-to-heart talk with yourself about making selling your life's work:

"Am I looking for an easy way to make a living?"

"Am I turning to selling because I can't think of anything else to do?"

"Am I selling because I think it's one field somebody without preparation can enter?"

"Am I just going to give it a try and see how it works out?"

You will not be ready for success as a salesman until you can look at yourself and the world and say, "The one thing I would rather be than anything else is a salesman, and I intend to be the best salesman in my field."

MARCH 19th
REPEAT, REPEAT, REPEAT

Any salesman, strange as it may sound, can increase his sales by telling himself as frequently as possible that he is going to increase his sales.

Repetition is the fundamental rhythm of all progress, the cadence of the universe.

It's the repeated explosions that generate power in the automobile engine. It's the constant surging of water against the turbine blades that generates electrical power. It's the constant and determined effort that breaks down all resistance, sweeps away all obstacles.

Repetition of positive thoughts will have the same effect on selling as did Franklin Roosevelt's on the belief that he would over come infantile paralysis. In a letter to a doctor, he said, "More important than most therapy is a belief on the patient's part that he WILL recover."

Here we have a wonderful example of the magic of believing.

MARCH 20th

MAKE IT CLEAR

Almost everyone is suspicious of vague ideas, complex mechanisms, half-explained facts. There is a strong tendency to reject altogether the vague, the complicated, the hard to understand.

People will buy merchandise when they realize and visualize a need for it. They will accept and act upon an idea when they can clearly understand how it will fit into their daily lives and help them.

In order to sell anything, therefore, you have to be able to give a customer a clear-cut, definite picture of just what is and how it will serve his needs and wants.

And before you can do that, naturally, you first have to have the clear-cut picture in your own mind. So although "know your product" may sound like a trite slogan, it's a basic bit of advice that can't be skipped over in any talk on selling.

MARCH 21st

THE PLUMBER AND THE PIPE

Knowledge pays off.

Take, for instance, the case of the plumber who fixed a leaky pipe with one tap of a hammer and sent a bill for $50 for services rendered. When asked to itemize this seemingly exorbitant charge for a minute or so of work, he sent a statement as follows:

"For hitting pipe with hammer: $1.00

"For knowing where to hit pipe: $49.00

"Total: $50.00"

We have every right to expect a man to know his business if he expects us to have any dealings with him. When we consult a doctor about a minor ailment, he doesn't have to put to use all the medical education he's absorbed on bones, glands and organs of the human body. But if we couldn't count on his having that kind of education we wouldn't have called him in the first place.

MARCH 22nd

THE UPPERDOG

I feel it's time for someone to stand up and say, "I'm for the upperdog!" I'm for the one who sets out to do something and does it; the one who recognizes the problems at hand and endeavors to deal with them; the one who isn't blaming someone else's failings...

The quality of any society is directly related to the quality of the individuals who make it up. We will never create a good society, much less a great one, until individual excellence and achievement are not only respected but encouraged.

Building a better society will only be done by those who take seriously their responsibility for making the most of their native ability, for getting the job done.

That is why I am for the achiever -- the succeeder -- the upperdog.

MARCH 23rd

THOUGHTS TO PONDER

Remember: There is no good thing in the world that is not available to you if you sufficiently desire it.

Cherish your visions and your dreams. They are the children of your soul, and blueprints of your ultimate achievements.

Know your own mind -- life your own life.

He who follows others is always behind; have the courage of your own originality.

Killing time is not murder; it is suicide.

Any fool can learn from experience -- it takes a wise man to learn from others.

Most salesmen would be glad to succeed by hard work -- if it did not take so much effort

MARCH 24th

REASONS TO FAIL

There never was a 100 percent perfect salesman who closed every sale, and there never will be. But you can steadily increase your "batting average" if, whenever you lose a sale, you will ask yourself, honestly, What did I do, or fail to do, which caused this sale to slip to my fingers?"

Did I see the right man, or an assistant?

Did I time my call to suit the buyer's convenience?

Did I take the trouble to learn something about the prospect before I called?

Did I get the buyer's full attention?

Did I listen patiently when he wanted to talk?

Did I present my proposition clearly and confidently?

Was I over-anxious?

Was I too hurried?

Did I fail to radiate enthusiasm?

MARCH 25th

FIVE LITTLE WORDS

The five words "attention, interest, conviction, desire, close" are the outline of a sales presentation familiar to most salesmen.

The salesman's main purpose should be to tell his story as clearly, effectively, honestly and briefly as possible. A well-organized selling format can grasp the customer's mind and carry it along without giving the prospect a chance to think of opposing ideas.

When the salesman does a good job of telling his story with an organized selling plan, he has an excellent chance of getting a "yes" answer.

No one likes to make decisions. Making a decision means change -- we expose ourselves to risk, and we hesitate and resist changing the existing conditions. The buyer pays for your best efforts in helping him to buy what will be best for him. Making the decision easy to make is certainly a big part of the service you can help him with.

MARCH 26th

WHY DID I LOSE THAT SALE?

Did I see the right man?

Did I take the trouble before calling to learn something about the prospect's business?

Did I get the buyer's full attention?

Did I listen patiently when he wanted to do the talking?

Did I have all the facts about my proposition?

Did I tell my complete sales story?

Did I present my proposition clearly and confidently?

Did I back down (and out) when the buyer said "No"?

Did I fail to ask "Why?" when he stated his objections?

Did I time my call to suit the buyer's convenience?

Did I show by my manner that I was afraid of not getting the order?

Was I over-anxious?

MARCH 27th

WHY DID I LOSE THAT SALE? (PART 2)

Did I demonstrate and prove my proposition?

Did I let him see, feel, taste, smell, operate and thoroughly examine my product?

Did I frequently remind him of the benefits of buying now?

When he said "Not interested" did I use the "But" technique or did I consider the interview at an end?

Was I too hurried in getting my story across?

Did I knock a competitor?

Did I really know the answers to all of his objections and questions?

Was I gossipy?

Did I fail to radiate enthusiasm and confidence?

Was I personally offensive in any way?

MARCH 28th

HELP THE PROSPECT MAKE A DECISION

It is important for the salesman to always keep in mind that his main job to help the prospect make the decision.

No one likes to make decisions. Making a decision means change--we expose ourselves to risk, and we hesitate and resist changing the existing conditions.

But if you present your proposition and don't follow through by sticking with the prospect until he makes a decision, you might be doing him a greater disservice than never to have called on him in the first place.

One important force we have going for us in selling is that the customer wants to believe we can help him.

Just the other day I used the personal appeal in closing.

"Mr. Buster, do you have enough confidence in me to let me set the promotion up the way I know it should be run?"

The fervent reply was, "My God, that's what I am depending on!"

MARCH 29th

LIVE FOR TODAY

As I get older I become aware of the folly of this perpetual reaching after The future, and of drawing from tomorrow, and from tomorrow only, a reason for the joyfulness of today.

I learned when, alas, it was almost too late, to live each moment as it passed over my head.

The greatest gift is the realization that life does not consist either of wallowing in the past or peering anxiously at the future.

Life is now, this day, this hour.

Enjoy your life without comparing it with that of others.

To be happy at home is the ultimate ambition, and the crowning achievement of success

MARCH 30th

LOYALTY COMES FIRST

Col. Willard F. Rockwell built two business empires simultaneously from scratch--Rockwell Standard Corp., a manufacturer of automotive parts, materials handling equipment and cotton gins, and North American Aviation, a manufacturer of executive aircraft.

He was asked, "How do you choose and keep the right men in the right jobs?"

He answered, "The qualities I look for above all are loyalty, belief in the company's growth ability and willingness to work and cooperate with people."

Please note: He placed loyalty first among the qualities he looks for in a man.

MARCH 31st

A VALUABLE JOB

There is no such thing as a job without importance. Every task, no matter how small, is necessary to the betterment and survival of mankind.

The salesman is, perhaps, able to find such fulfillment more readily than the average person because he is not only able to claim the position of medium between manufacturer and buyer, he is also the connecting link that keeps the worker at his job.

Without salesmen it wouldn't seek likely that many time cards would be punched or production would remain at a balanced pace.

If the time is given to take an inventory of the situation, the salesman will discover that his efforts are felt in areas he never suspected and that his sense of worth is far more established than previously realized.

Selling is an art, a physical accomplishment and a mental conquest. It is not work for the weak, nor is it a job for the irresponsible.

APRIL 1st

MANAGER OR PUPPET?

All too often owners or general managers who hire sales managers forget what the word "manager" means and keep their sales managers on strings, never delegating to them the authority they need to really do their jobs.

The outcome is that the owner or general manager pokes his nose into too many jobs that aren't his immediate province. The sales manager loses his initiative and the salesmen become demoralized.

Once you have appointed your sales manager, give him the authority he needs--or better still, more than he needs--and let him carry the ball. I don't mean you should turn your business over to him, but rather you should keep your responsibilities distinct from his.

APRIL 2nd

NO WAITING

The person who waits for things to turn up has his eyes fixed on his toes.

Here are some suggested actions to help you step up your effectiveness as a salesman:

* Learn at least 3 reasons why a prospect needs your product.

* Watch your health; visit your doctor for a check-up periodically.

* Be sincere; learn what you need to know and don't bluff.

* Put your merchandise in the hands of the prospect.

* Ask for the order!

APRIL 3rd

A NEW VISION

By changing your point of view for a day, you can often open your eyes and see yourself and your behavior in a new light.

Go through an entire day as if you were about to leave the job or the community.

Go through a day imagining the questions a 12-year-old might ask about your way of responding to common situations.

Spend a day alone, with no fixed program.

Examine new byways. Take a new route even if it's only on the way to work.

Take a trip back to your old home town and search out remembered landmarks.

Imagine that you and one of your subordinates have switched roles. How would he act?

APRIL 4th

THAT DIRTY WORD

A large percentage of the friction between salesmen and the office is caused by that dirty word, reports.

Generally speaking, salesman are not good detail men. They dislike writing reports. Their attitude is, "I could be putting in my time better selling." Better be reconciled to the fact that selling is more than an 8 hour a day, 40 hours a week job.

Reports are important to you as well as to the office.

They are your main means of communication with headquarters, telling them how you are spending the time they are paying you for.

After you've tried it for a while, writing reports becomes easier.

Just don't fight your work.

APRIL 5th

LET THE PROSPECT HAVE HIS HEAD

If you ever observed an expert horseman on a spirited animal you would note he lets the horse "have his head" and seldom forces him, but all the time the reins are held tight by the trained hands of the rider.

The horse is doing exactly what the master wants, and is happy.

Old pros in selling will tell you that many of their big sales were the result of the customer making up his own mind. In the customer's mind he BOUGHT...he was not SOLD.

Lead the customer to the point of closing, then help him make up his own mind to buy.

APRIL 6th

A FEW SELLING TIPS

Make each day a full selling day.

Determine that you will not let disappointments sour you.

Go to your prospect expecting to sell. Don't go in to visit.

Approach your prospect with a well-planned idea.

Get sincerely interested in your prospect and his problems.

Get out if the prospect shows signs of boredom or preoccupation.

Dodge any bait for an argument with a customer.

Put every failure through your own mental laboratory. Try to discover how and why you failed.

APRIL 7th

A MATTER OF GUTS

Even during the terrible depression of 1929-32 there were a lot of companies that made a profit because their salesmen had the "guts" to not only keep on fighting for orders but to fight harder than ever.

If this had not been the case, practically every company in America would have gone out of business.

The great depression of the '30s proved again that every battle ever fought in selling has been won by the men who refused to be licked by whatever was opposing them, whether it was recession, depression, competition, that mythical thing called "conditions" or the "international situation."

When it's all said and done the only thing that can lick you or any other salesman is fearful thinking.

APRIL 8th

WHAT MAKES PROFITS

Get the following idea firmly planted in your mind, because it is fundamental--you just can't escape it:

"Business profits do not come from making things, but come from selling the things that business makes."

Perhaps that's why so many presidents of successful companies in America were at one time those companies' best salesmen. You've got to be good to sell. Not just good now and then, but good all the time.

APRIL 9th

THE FEAR FACTOR

Fear, the greatest of all human weaknesses, has kept the majority of people out of selling.

They just can't imagine themselves going around with a briefcase containing a mysterious assortment of material, trying to get in to see buyers and induce them to order the material.

Salesmen have embraced a brand of self-confidence that insists you can survive and be successful in spite of fear.

The beginning salesman dreads making his first call. The old-timer has one particular call he is afraid to make; somebody there dislikes him, is out to get him.

Fear comes to all men. The best way is to face it, wrestle with it, take it apart and tear it to pieces.

Courage is something that can be studied, practiced, learned and finally captured. There can be no self-confidence without such courage.

APRIL 10th

TIME IS MONEY

It is important to use your time judiciously. The most profitable hours are those you spend in actual selling or telling the story of your product.

Obviously, those "story telling" hours are not going to yield their money's worth to you unless the calls you make produce a commensurate volume of business.

You must shorten as far as possible the time spent on accounts that do not produce a comparable dollar value to time required in calling on them.

Time is measured against net sales results.

The most valuable thing in the world is time--spend it wisely and the rewards will be great.

APRIL 11th

THE VALUE OF DISCONTENT

The salesman must be discontented.

It is only when a man is NEVER satisfied that he can succeed as a salesman.

If every salesman wanted just "his share" and no more, there's be no progress, no prosperity, no profit -- and no company for very long.

It is salesmen who want their share AND the other fellow's, salesmen who aren't satisfied until they get it, who build business.

Every man who is worthy to be called a salesman should adopt this slogan:

"There is not enough business in my entire territory to satisfy me."

The man who has the priceless ingredient of self-motivation possesses the driving force that will carry him to success.

APRIL 12th

ON LEADERSHIP

Leadership is definable. However, it is too complex to ever be reduced to one or two precise traits. To define leadership, we must first break it down to its components:

First, the elements or qualities or leadership can be developed. The statement "Leaders are made, not born" seems clearly proven by a study of leadership.

Second, practically every salesman has within him some of the basic elements of leadership: desire for achievement, mental energy, decisiveness, persistence, confidence, integrity, persuasiveness and the ability to handle people.

No two individuals are the same regarding what might be called the "combined package"; each has a somewhat different degree of development of the component factors.

APRIL 13th

CREATIVE SALESMANSHIP

A creative salesman presumes that there is a need for one or more of his products in every place of business he calls on. Acting on this resumption, he turns up business where "it just couldn't exist."

Making certain that your customer is getting the fullest value out of what you sold him is your best protection against losing him to a competitor. Also, a customer who is not making the best use of what he bought from you is a poor prospect for repeat sales or sales of other products in your line.

You can't afford to sell him and forget him. You must create the opportunities to test whether he is making the best use of your product.

The simplest way is to make a service call and ask how your product is working out. Pass an idea along to your customer that helps him get more value out of the product. It can be an idea you picked up from another customer who is enjoying the product fully.

APRIL 14th
NEW BUSINESS

New business is usually opened up in one of two ways. It can be obtained by closing a previously unsold account in a competitive field formerly serviced by someone else.Or it can be developed by finding additional outlets or sources of distribution in untapped areas.

In the first instance you simply take over a competitive account. In the second instance, however, if you can find new uses for the product the entire field is enlarged.

The history of the Waring Blender illustrates the value of finding new outlets for a product. It was first introduced shortly before World War II, chiefly to crack ice for mixed drinks in bars. But they appealed instantly to research chemists for making laboratory emulsions. And today no well-organized kitchen is complete unless it includes some type of household blender.

The blender is a good example of how developing new uses for a product can pyramid its sales.

APRIL 15th
WHO PAYS FOR DAYS OFF?

What happens when you don't show up for work for just one day?

Two people pay dearly: your employer and you!

Most of all, you.

Unessential absence, that "one day" triggered by a "what-difference-does-it-make?" attitude, multiplied by other employees' absences, disrupts business, delays orders, irritates customers and reduces profits.

What if you're really sick, and should be in bed? In that case, the last place the boss wants you to be is at your post. He doesn't want to delay your quick recovery. Your employer is not looking for martyrs. All he wants is a fair shake for his money. The same as you would want for yours.

APRIL 16th

TALKING TURKEY

"Cold turkey" canvassing can make money for you no matter what your line may be. More calls mean more prospects. Prospecting separates the salesmen from the order takers.

Even with the best salesman, prospecting can be real drudgery at times. But it must be done or he will be out of business. It is as simple as that.

No prospecting, no new business.

Open the telephone book and there are your prospects to call on. People are willing to tell you they are interested in your products, if you will give them a chance.

Ask them to buy, tell them about your fill line of products. You will be amazed at the results.

APRIL 17th

LOOKING GOOD

The modern salesman must be physically fit -- not only to satisfy the physical and mental demands of his strenuous work, but also because of the direct influence of good physical condition on his mental attitude and personal appearance.

A clean, neat, well-groomed appearance and pleasant expression are the result of good health.

If a salesman looks attractive, he makes a good initial impression and receives a favorable reception -- so essential in effective personal relationship with buyers

APRIL 18th

MANNERS MATTER

Good manners are a distinguishing characteristic of the most successful salesman. By having respect for the opinions of others, by recognizing their accomplishments and overlooking their shortcomings you gain their favorable consideration.

Consideration for others, expressed by such phrases as "Would you mind?" or "I'm sorry to trouble you," enables a salesman to make his relations with prospects and customers pleasant and profitable.

The characteristics of a successful salesman include sincerity, self-confidence, enthusiasm, courtesy, imagination, initiative, honesty, tact, loyalty, resourcefulness and a genuine liking for people.

APRIL 19th

KNOW YOUR COMPETITION

More sales and profits have been lost because of a lack of up-to-date information than because of poor judgment. And one of the most fruitful sources of information is often overlooked because it's so close: the competition.

Management usually knows what the competition has done in the past, but may not know enough about what it is doing at the moment and is likely to do in the future. Without this information, many marketing decisions become haphazard.

How much do you know about your competitors?

APRIL 20th

QUALITY Vs. PRICE

You don't have to lower your prices to close sales. There is always a lower price than yours. Successful salesman don't talk just price, they talk about quality.

Remember this: every company knows what its product is worth and sells it accordingly.

People will buy quality when they are approached intelligently. Don't just say, "My product is better." Show them; let them compare.

There is no such thing as a quality product for the price of an inferior item

APRIL 21st

MAKE IT LAST

Anyone can see the advantage of taking care of his car, his home, his golf clubs, his fishing tackle. They last longer. Remember, the same thing is true of the equipment you work with.

When a company buys a piece of equipment it estimates what the normal life of that equipment should be. The company then charges off a certain percent of its cost each year. This process is called depreciation.

When equipment is abused, when it wears out faster than the company has estimated, it is necessary for them to get the money for the new equipment somewhere else.

Where do they get the money? Out of profits.

If doesn't take too many careless employees to wipe out profits entirely.

APRIL 22nd

THINK BIG

Too much thinking is little, not big.

All around you is an environment trying to pull you down Second Class Street.

You are told almost daily that there are "too many chiefs and not enough Indians." In other words, that opportunities to lead no longer exist, that there is a surplus of chiefs, so be content to be a little guy.

This petty environment tells you "Whatever will be will be;" that "Your destiny is outside your control;" that "Fate is in complete control." So forget those dreams; lie down and wait to die because success isn't worth the price.

But, in truth, success doesn't demand a price. Every step forward pays a dividend. Start now, right now, to discover how to make your thinking make success for you.

Life is too short to be little.

APRIL 23rd

YOUR PARACHUTE

The salesman has a surprising similarity to a parachute jumper! Before the jumper makes that step into the void, he goes through a period of ground training. And for new jumpers, a static line attached to the plane automatically jerks open the chute.

The salesman making his first call at an office or store has usually had initial training to help him know the ropes. The salesman has his own static line. He depends on what others have said and done to establish his own routine.

Just as the jumper must dispense with the static line and make a free fall, the salesman must find his own techniques, develop his own ways of meeting prospects and making sales.

And just as the jumper has an emergency chute, the salesman has one too.

He calls his FAITH.

APRIL 24th

PROSPECT OR PERISH

If the title sounds grim, it was meant to. You can't stay alive in selling unless you systematically go after new accounts.

Too many salesmen regard a territory as a lifetime sinecure that will yield good earnings without cultivation. This is a fallacy.

A territory must be exploited or it will dry up on you.

The key word is "systematic." There must be a pattern to your prospecting.

Depending on hit-or-miss tips, one-shot cold calls, etc., is dangerous. A certain amount of screening is called for. A lot of time can be wasted on buyers who really aren't prospects at all -- at least not for YOUR product.

APRIL 25th

BIG BASS FISHING

There is a type of salesman who is unsparing of his energy for prospecting, but he is fishing for minnows when he should be casting for big-mouth bass.

This is known as the small account complex. A man devotes a great deal of time to cold calling and tracking down leads, but he stays away from the big account.

Subconsciously, he avoids the large customer in his prospecting. Why?

The answer is simple: the big buyer is harder to sell.

The salesman knows he's going to have a tough fight and he's afraid to start slugging. Don't let the size of the prospect deter you. No matter how big they are, somebody is buying and he has a "hot button." If you are not pressing it, your competitor is.

APRIL 26th

A MATTER OF PRIDE

Don't let yourself be cowered or intimidated by the buyer.

Don't even appear too grateful for the interview. Instead make him feel that he's been selected by you; that you are giving him YOUR time.

Give him the impression that you don't pick prospects at random, but only after careful consideration. Make him feel that he's a blue-chip choice.

This will tickle his pride.

Be polite, observe the usual amenities, but don't get down on your knees and bow in gratitude.

And come away with an order!

APRIL 27th

KNOW YOUR PRODUCT

Brush up on the product that you are selling -- as though you were just starting our and didn't know anything at all about it.

Find out all over again what "makes it tick" -- what its competitive advantages are -- just WHY anybody should buy it -- especially in preference to your nearest competitor's product.

Don't be satisfied until you're absolutely sure that you know why your project is better than any competitor's, and that you know how to prove it.

APRIL 28th

THE THRILL OF SELLING

Selling is not only the profit producing end of business, it is the fighting end of business, too -- a steady, thrilling challenge to men who love to see a business grow; to whom there is no greater satisfaction than seeing a territory blossom and expand, under the magic touch of intelligent salesmanship.

There is no reason why any salesman in any company should be anything but optimistic about his and his company's future as long as he remembers that...

"We sell or we sink," and as long as he backs up that truism with intelligent sales activity on the firing line.

APRIL 29th

THE GOLFER'S WAY

The way to become a proficient salesman parallels that of becoming a good golfer.

Lessons from a pro are helpful. You can also pick up a lot of pointers by watching a golf matches on TV.

But the only way you can really improve your game is through practice, practice, practice.

So it is with selling. The only way you can become a professional salesman is through practice, practice, practice.

It is not something that is done to you. It is something you do to yourself.

APRIL 30th

LIVE IN THE PRESENT

Many people have the idea that all training should be directed at some future job. This is folly for three reasons:

First we never can know what the future really holds for us. In our growing economy, opportunities appear one day that we can't possibly foresee.

Secondly, the only yardstick that can be used to measure your ability to handle a bigger assignment is your performance on your present assignment.

And thirdly, doing a better all-around job now will bring you not only increased income and prestige, but also pride and confidence plus satisfaction.

MAY 1st

WHAT WENT WRONG?

One of the best producers I know uses this checklist after an unproductive call, asking himself:

"Would the prospect have benefited from the purchase?"

"What did he lose by not buying?"

"Did the man I called on have the authority to buy?"

"Did I tell the prospect the whole story, covering all points in the proper sequence, despite interruptions?"

"Did I speak in terms of benefits that meant something to him?"

"Did I listen carefully when he talked?"

MAY 2nd

WHAT WENT WRONG, PART II

Here are more questions a top producer I know uses after an unproductive calls. He asks himself:

"Did the prospect present any major objections that I was unable to handle with finesse?"

"Was I able to answer his questions without bluffing?"

"Did I give up really trying to sell him the first time he said no?"

"Did I specifically ask him for an order? How many times?"

"Should I ask my supervisor for help or criticism?"

MAY 3rd

EVALUATE YOURSELF

A salesman should ask himself these questions:

"How good am I in price negotiations?"

"How adequate are my follow-ups on new or prospective customers?"

"Do I furnish complete information with each new credit order?"

"Do I keep my division manager informed of the activities in my territory?"

"How well do I know our product? Related products?"

"How well do I know the company, its objectives, organization and management philosophy?"

MAY 4th

EVALUATE YOURSELF, PART II

More questions a salesman should ask himself:

"Does my appearance appeal to the customer?"

"Do I have annoying habits?"

"Can I think under pressure?"

"Can I speak my mind against opposition?"

"Am I determined to succeed?"

"Can I accept and use constructive criticism?"

"Do I enjoy the competitive side of selling?"

MAY 5th
EVALUATE YOURSELF, PART III

More questions a salesman should ask himself:

"Do I act on my own initiative?"

"Do I originate new ideas and methods?"

"Do I do more than is required?"

"Do I seek out responsibility?"

"Do I put in a full day's work?"

"Do I spend my own time in self-improvement?"

MAY 6th
EVALUATE YOURSELF, PART IV

More questions a salesman should ask himself:

"Do I see my own responsibility and relationship with others in the organization?"

"Do I recognize my responsibilities for good relations with customers, suppliers and the public?"

"Am I generally respected by my associates?"

"Am I active in community affairs? Trade associations?"

"Can I express myself well?"

"Can I argue without being antagonistic?"

MAY 7th
EVALUATE YOURSELF, PART V

More questions a salesman should ask himself:

"Do I put forth the necessary effort each day?"

"Did I take full advantage of the sales promotions put on by my company?"

"Did I use all of the sales helps provided me by my company to the best of my ability?"

"Have I really put in a few extra hours each week seeking out new business?"

"How many new customers have I added?"

MAY 8th
YOUR ASSISTANT -- THE MANUFACTURER

Many salesmen struggle along without ever putting to use the most valuable sales assistant they have -- the manufacturer of the product you are selling.

It pays to know everything there is to know about the product -- all of its features, how and why it is superior to the competition, how it specifically appeals to different types of people.

Design and packaging are most important today; take time to study such details. Know all about the advertising your company has done.

MAY 9th

JOIN THE TEAM

You will not reach the top in your profession if you are not a team worker.

I don't care how good you are, this truth is for you.

Knute Rockne had one of the great backfields of all time in the legendary Four Horsemen of Notre Dame's 1924 team. But one day, in the last quarter of a game already won, he took out his first-string line and substituted the third-string line.

For that quarter the Four Horsemen were stopped cold. They learned their lesson. What was winning games for Notre Dame was a whole team, not four supermen.

The superman is made by the teamwork of his fellow players. The same thing is true in selling.

MAY 10th

YOU AND YOUR COMPANY

Some employees give no thought whatsoever to the well-being, success and growth of the company that pays their wages.

They seem to feel that their paychecks are their due, whether they did anything to earn them or not.

If management is to be concerned with the well-being of its employees, it is certainly only fair that employees be concerned with the well-being of the company they're expecting to pay their rent, buy their clothes and food and send their kids to school.

Any person who looks to industry for his security, without understanding that each of us must earn it for himself, is a fool.

And sooner or later, it is inevitable that this person will find himself on the outside looking in.

MAY 11th

THE HUMAN VACUUM CLEANER

I know a man who is a tremendous asset to his organization, because he invariable demonstrates a triumphant thought pattern.

If his associates view a proposition pessimistically, he employs what he called "the vacuum cleaner method" -- that is, by a series of questions he "sucks the dust" out of his associates' minds; he draws out their negative attitudes, then quietly suggests positive ideas about the proposition until a new set of attitudes gives them a new concept of the facts.

It's his confident attitude that makes the difference.

MAY 12th

SEVEN IS A WINNING NUMBER

These are your greatest assets, and worth striving for:

1. A wonderful wife.

2. Devoted children who will stand by you.

3. Friends who will help you and who hold you in esteem.

4. Integrity; it's nothing to be ashamed of.

5. Good physical health.

6. Living in the United States, the greatest country in the world.

7. Religious faith.

MAY 13th

FIRST, SELL YOURSELF

The first sale every salesman must make is to sell himself the idea that salesmanship is to be his life's work.

Nobody should choose selling as his profession who would be happier doing something else, or who is not prepared to put into it everything he has.

You will not be ready for success until you can look at yourself and say, "The one thing I would rather be than anything else is a salesman, and I intend to be the best salesman in my field."

MAY 14th

A DAY'S WORK

The dictionary is the only place where "success" comes before "work."

Many fail to recognize opportunity because its favorite disguise is hard work.

The man who is content to "get by" is the man who will be passed by.

Twenty companies were asked to state the distinguishing good qualities of their most successful salesmen. The answers put good character at the top of the list. But immediately after that was "willingness to do a full day's work."

MAY 15th

RABBIT HUNTING

An old-time salesman told me how he consistently tripled his sales quota:

See the people.

Apply your product to your people's needs.

Tell its story.

Close the sale.

This reminds me of a recipe for rabbit pie in an old English cookbook that starts "First, catch the rabbit."

The first step in salesmanship is "First, find a customer."

The only way to catch a rabbit is to get out into the fields. The only way to find a customer is to get out and makes calls.

MAY 16th

SOMETHING EXTRA

There is all the difference in the world between the man who says, "Well, I guess I have done enough today" and the man who says, "I need a least one more sale today to keep up with the goal I have set myself."

This man makes the extra call -- that little extra call every day, which means 250 every year -- and registers its effect in extra accomplishment

MAY 17th

SOME THOUGHTS FOR SALESMEN

Any fool can learn from experience -- it takes a wise man to learn from others.

Most salesmen would be glad to succeed by hard work if it did not take so much effort.

The swiftest salesman can never outrun opportunity in the United States of America.

Expect to make sales, but do not expect them to make themselves.

MAY 18th

MORE THOUGHTS FOR SALESMEN

The salesman who only pops off will pop out.

Sales ability gets a customer; service ability keeps him.

Credit for service pays off in cash.

The worst buy in the world is an alibi.

The man who clips customers cuts his own life line.

MAY 19th

THE MEDIUM IS **NOT** THE MESSAGE

For those above the level of manual labor, skill in communication is one of the important reasons we are employed for any position.

For salespeople, it is THE reason.

Methods of communication have made startling advances in the past few years, but attention has been focused chiefly on scientific accomplishments.

Not enough consideration has been given to WHAT is being transmitted.

A company may have the best product of its kind, but if the salesmen do not get across to prospects its value, use and need, it will not be sold and used with profit by the customers.

MAY 20th

THE SECRET WEAPON

If each salesman will put as much time and attention toward perfecting his sales presentation as has gone into developing new spectacular methods of communication, he will have great awards.

His greatest asset, his secret weapon, is his command of English.

He can make it work for him with extraordinary success.

The salesman's formal education may be much or little, his intellectual powers great or small, but if he gets the right thoughts out of his head into the heats of his customers and prospects he will have earnings far above the average

MAY 21st
CONNECT ALL PLUGS

The average salesman wouldn't think of driving his car with only a few of the spark plugs connected, because he knows it would only sputter along.

Why should so many salesmen sputter through their sales presentation with several of their mental spark plugs disconnected?

It may indicate carelessness, lack of ambition to do a better job, or mental laziness.

The lack of effective communications hinders advancement, especially in salesmanship.

Give mind service, instead of lip service, to the importance of communication

MAY 22nd

ECONOMIC LITERACY

Look at the following list of topics and determine what you know about each:

City manager forms of government

Credit buying

Federal aid to education

Labor unions

Taxation

Farm problems

Bond elections

National debt

Too often our salesmen's comments are limited to "Taxes are too darn high," or "Why don't they pay teachers more money?"

The effectiveness of government depends on the understanding of its people.

Let's improve our economic literacy.

MAY 23rd

WHERE OTHERS FEAR TO TREAD

Salesmen are by nature aggressive, constructive, out-going, happy individuals. This is their inclination as salesmen.

If their over-confidence sometimes gets them in trouble, they can be forgiven; their job is to make things happen when others hold back fearfully.

Let us never forget that communities have been built, industries located, businesses established and civic improvements started by individuals whose optimism, courage -- or foolhardiness, call it what you will -- caused them to go ahead at a time when others shrank in pessimism and fear.

MAY 24th

TAKE A BREAK

The Pan-American Coffee Bureau surveyed nearly 1,200 companies, large medium and small, and found that 82 percent reported a reduction in worker fatigue due to the coffee break; 75 percent reported better employee morale, and 62 percent saw an increase in worker productivity.

Alcoholic beverages may produce a short-lived stimulation, but it fades away quickly and people feel more tired that before.

Coffee, tea, and, to a lesser degree, cocoa are very effective stimulants.

A coffee break in the afternoon can mean relaxation and relief.

MAY 25th

ARE YOU LOYAL?

What is this thing called "loyalty?"

It is one of the most valuable assets that any individual or business can possess, and yet:

You can't buy it;

You can't borrow it;

You can't inherit it;

You can't give it away.

It never appears in the assets column of a company's financial statement, but without loyalty on the part of its employees, executive and owners, no business can be truly and permanently successful.

MAY 26th

THE FEW, THE LOYAL

The other day I asked the personnel director of a local company, "About how many people work at your place now?"

"Oh," he replied, "about 15 to 20 percent."

Then he shook his head, sighed and said, "I wish we had more like them -- they are the loyal ones."

It's sad but true -- today too many so-called working people don't want to work; all they really want is to get the paycheck and the fringe benefits.

To them "loyalty" is a much abused and misused word, like "service" and "quality."

MAY 27th
THE WORKING MAN'S CREED

1. I believe that an ounce of loyalty is worth a carload of half-hearted effort.

2. I believe in the company I am working for, and in my own ability to measure up to the responsibilities of my job.

3. I believe in the work I am doing, and in the excellence of the products and service I am helping to produce and sell.

MAY 28th
THE WORKING MAN'S CREED, PART II

4. I believe that honest, loyal effort is the foundation on which all true success is built.

5. I believe in working, not wishing; in complimenting, not condemning; in gratitude for the privilege of my job, not in complaining about its requirements.

6. I believe that everyone gets what he deserves and that our tomorrows are the result of what we think and do today.

MAY 29th

THE WORKING MAN'S CREED, PART III

7. I believe in my company's customers, and their right to expect and receive the best work of which I am capable.

8. I believe in courtesy, consideration and helpfulness to those loyal fellow workers who daily help me to do a good job.

9. I believe that no one can be a failure unless he has lost faith in himself, and in the value of honest work.

10. I believe that loyalty to my company comes FIRST in my job.

MAY 30th

THE PLAGUE OF COMPLACENCY

Webster's definition of complacency: "Pleased, contentment, smugness, self-satisfaction."

My definition: "Easy way, lack of interest, no ambition, lead poison (and NOT in the blood stream)."

Statistics prove that more businesses fail from the sin of complacency that any other reason.

When a company or a salesman become satisfied with the results of his efforts, he is signing his own business death warrant.

MAY 31st

CONSUMERS IN CONTROL

In the final analysis the consumer is the ultimate judge of what stays on grocers' shelves.

One of the most widely repeated phrases in the food industry, whether it applies to a product or a practice, is: "The consumer won't accept it."

To attract and hold the wily and fickle shopper, supermarkets must have a good image in all areas -- meat, produce, checkout, etc.

While consumers want convenience in products, they resist items that are TOO convenient, that take away the opportunity to create.

Remember, the consumer is discriminating -- and demanding.

JUNE 1st

ATTITUDE MAKES A DIFFERENCE

Attitude makes a difference in job performance and in whether or not a person is successful.

Dictionaries define attitude as "a state of mind that is revealed by our behavior or conduct, which demonstrates our purpose or opinion regarding some matter."

I sometimes think of it as putting a little of ourselves in our work, over and above the skill necessary to perform it.

We are already being monetarily compensated for our work; it is this little extra which attracts recognition and pays off in inner satisfaction.

JUNE 2nd

R's and A's

We know about the three R's of the classroom, but there are also the three R's of adult life:

Resources: training and other gifts we offer;

Resolution: what we decided to do with our resources;

Responsibility: the sincerity of purpose we put into life.

There are also three A's of business life:

Ability: establishes what a worker does, and will bring him a paycheck.

Ambition: determines how much he does, and will get him a raise.

Attitude: guarantees how well he does.

JUNE 3rd

WHY WAIT?

Machines move mountains; initiative moves men.

You've seen it yourself. There are two kinds of people in the world: the waiters and the doers.

The waiter thinks about how things could be better.

The doer works to make them better.

The only way to beat the waiting game is by getting started.

Stop merely intending to take action. Seize the opportunity and do something. Get started -- then finish it.

You have only one lifetime to use. It's slipping by minute by minute.

Be a doer, not a waiter.

JUNE 4th

HANDLING SUCCESS

Success for an individual or a business is a matter of never-ceasing application. You must forever work at it diligently. Otherwise it takes wings and flies away.

At no time can you afford to rest on your laurels -- a pause for self-admiration -- because there are others who may have eyes on your coveted place and who would like nothing better than to push you out of it, especially if they observe that you have a weak hold on it or are doing nothing to strengthen your position.

JUNE 5th

THE PROBLEM OF FEAR

Are you afraid to take on responsibilities, afraid to make decisions, afraid to step out alone?

Most people are -- that's why there are so few leaders and so many followers.

If you are confronted with a problem, the longer you put if off, the greater it becomes and the more fearful you become of your ability to solve it.

Therefore, learn to make decisions, because in not deciding you invite failure.

JUNE 6th

DECIDE AND ACT

Experience will soon teach you that once a decision is made, the problems and troubles begin to disappear. Even though the decision you make may not be the best one, the mere deciding gives you strength and raises your morale.

Decide and act, and the chances are that your troubles will fade into thin air -- whether you make a mistake or not.

Learn to be quick in making decisions and audacious in your actions.

JUNE 7th

DEALING WITH PEOPLE

Various studies have proven that if you learn how to deal with other people, you will have gone about 85 percent of the way down the road to success in any business, occupation or profession, and about 99 percent of the way down the road to personal happiness.

One study found that for every one person who lost his job for failure to do the work, two persons lost their jobs for failure to deal successful with people.

Learn skill in dealing with people with confidence and you will automatically improve your success and happiness.

JUNE 8th

IMPORTANT PEOPLE

You want to make a good impression on the other fellow. But the most effective way ever discovered for impressing the other fellow is to let him know that you are impressed by HIM.

Don't underestimate small courtesies such as being on time for an appointment. It is by small things that we acknowledge the importance of the other person.

Remind yourself that other people ARE important, and your attitude will get across to the other person.

JUNE 9th

THE VALUE OF CONFIDENCE

A confident manner in a salesman is like having money in the bank.

Act confident, look confident, and you'll find that you begin to feel more confident. More important, your customers and prospective customers will begin to have more confidence in you.

I've seen mediocre salesmen make a good record because they knew how to act and talk in a confident manner.

Remember, if you believe in yourself and act as if you believe in yourself, others will believe in you.

JUNE 10th

BODY LANGUAGE

Our physical actions express our mental attitudes. If you see a man walking along with shoulders bent and drooped, you can know that his burdens are almost too heavy for him to bear.

See a man walking along with head down and eyes downcast, and you know he is feeling pessimistic.

A man with a feeling of confidence steps out boldly. His shoulders are back, and his eyes are looking out and up to some goal he feels he can attain.

JUNE 11th

LISTEN TO YOURSELF

We express ourselves through our voices more than in any other way.

The voice is the most highly developed means of communication between human beings.

But your voice communicates more than ideas. It also communicates your feelings about yourself.

Begin to listen to your own voice. Does it express hopelessness or courage?

Have you, without realizing it, gotten into the habit of talking in a whining way? Do you speak up confidently -- or mumble?

JUNE 12th

A GOOD START

In dealing with other people, you yourself sound the keynote for the entire theme, when you begin the interview.

If you start off on a note of formality, the meeting will be formal.

Start off on a note of friendliness and the meeting will be friendly.

Set the stage for a business-like discussion, and it will be business-like.

Start on a note of apology and the other person will force you to play that theme all the way through.

JUNE 13th

FIRST IMPRESSIONS

When you meet someone for the first time, the impression you make then is very likely to be the keynote that will determine how he regards you for the rest of your life.

Other people tend to accept you at your own evaluation. If you think you are a nobody, you are practically asking other people to snub you.

One of the best means ever discovered for impressing the other fellow favorably is not to strive too hard to make an impression, but to let him know that he is making a good impression on YOU.

JUNE 14th

WHAT'S YOUR OPINION?

People judge you not only by the opinion you hold of yourself, but also by the opinions you hold on other things: your job, your company, even your competition.

Negative opinions create a negative atmosphere. Don't be a knocker.

And don't be a sorehead.

The way in which you ask things, in itself, sets the stage or sounds the keynote for the other person.

Don't ask "No" questions if you want "Yes" answers.

Don't ask questions or issue instructions that imply you expect trouble.

Why ask for trouble?

JUNE 15th

GOOD AS GOLD

Every job is like a gold mine.

The more effort and skill you put into working the mine, the more gold you get out of it. Unless you work the mine, the gold stays buried in the ground.

We must give more to our jobs before we can get more out of them.

Too many people today look upon their jobs as a series of interludes between coffee breaks, rest periods, weekends, vacations and retirement.

Their attitude is "What do I get out of it?" instead of "What can I put into it?" -- and they they wonder why they are bypassed when promotions are handed out.

JUNE 16th

HOW TO INCREASE SALES

Rule 1: Maintain, at all times, a positive, constructive, progressive attitude toward your job, your company and your working associates.

Always think in terms of how things can be done -- never in terms of why they cannot. Such an attitude leads upward. An attitude of indifference can lead only to mediocrity and failure

JUNE 17th

HOW TO INCREASE SALES

Rule 2: Remember always that in the final analysis no one is ever paid LESS than he is worth -- for real value is ultimately recognized. If you thoroughly understand and believe this fact you, too, will discover that the best and only way to get more out of your job is to give more of yourself to it

JUNE 18th

HOW TO INCREASE SALES

Rule 3: Keep reminding yourself that you have two "bosses" to please -- (1) your company and (2) your company's customers.

In fact, (2) is the more important, for unless its customers are satisfied the company cannot long exist. Not matter what your job happens to be, it has a bearing on customer satisfaction -- directly or indirectly.

Your company's customers are its biggest asset. Without them there could be no company.

See that everything you do in your job has the customer in mind.

JUNE 19th

HOW TO INCREASE SALES

Rule 4: Be willing, at all times, to make any personal sacrifice in order to do whatever is required in the proper performance of your job.

Business, like marriage, is a matter of "give and take," and at times we all have to give a little more than usual -- and do it willingly without grumbling.

The bigger the job, the more one is called upon for such extra effort.

JUNE 20th

HOW TO INCREASE SALES

Rule 5: It pays to be profit-minded and to realize that not only your company's growth but your own future depends on the company making a proper profit.

Keep your eyes open for everything and anything, in connection with your work, which can reduce expenses, eliminate waste (of materials or time) or increase the company's income.

Often a simple change can be made which will greatly increase the profitability of an operation, and its sales volume.

JUNE 21st

HOW TO INCREASE SALES

Rule 6: Develop a cooperative team spirit that enables you not only to get along with other people, but to encourage and inspire them in their work.

As you succeed in doing this you will find yourself using the word "we" much more often than "I" and your work will have a new meaning for you.

JUNE 22nd

HOW TO INCREASE SALES

Rule 7: Problems arise in every job. Learn to face them head-on.

You cannot solve any problem by turning your back to it -- or thinking of excuses for putting off a decision.

The principal function of an executive is the making of decisions about problems that arise.

Don't fear problems -- face them.

They have a way of growing bigger the longer we shy away from them.

JUNE 23rd

HOW TO INCREASE SALES

Rule 8: Each job is important or it would not exist. Be sure that you realize this about YOUR job -- then study its meaning and importance to the company, and its relation to jobs higher up.

Your company wants to grow, just as you want to grow. But it cannot progress if everyone in the organization remains forever in the same spot.

Each of today's jobs is a stepping stone to a better job tomorrow for those workers who prove their value and their readiness to take the next step.

YOUR job is to sell more

JUNE 24th

HOW TO INCREASE SALES

Rule 9: Ideas are the seeds of progress -- for individuals, companies, communities and nations. You never know when an idea may come to you which could be of value to the company.

But ideas cannot penetrate a closed mind. So keep an open mind to new ideas and suggestions. Ask questions; read; study; observe.

Ideas are everywhere for those who are on the lookout for them.

JUNE 25th

HOW TO INCREASE SALES

Rule 10: There are two kinds of people in every business organization -- the Dawdlers and the Doers.

The Dawdlers try to put everything off until tomorrow.

The Doers do it TODAY, in order to get that much MORE accomplished tomorrow.

It pays to get things done. It not only gives you a satisfactory feeling of accomplishment, but it gives a lift to the spirit and morale of everyone around you.

Yes, get it done --TODAY.

Tomorrow will present its own problems.

JUNE 26th

HOW TO INCREASE SALES

Rule 11: Change is a product of the times, and a necessary element to growth -- in any business.

The people who advance, in a growing company, are those who WILLINGLY accept changes instead of assuming the attitude "We've never done it that way before!"

Welcome change, whenever it comes.

It shows that your company is alert to new ideas and methods.

JUNE 27th

HOW TO INCREASE SALES

Rule 12: Do whatever you do with enthusiasm.

A sincere spirit of enthusiasm in and for your work not only helps you, but it also inspires all who come in contact with you, for it is contagious. You can't fake enthusiasm -- it must be genuine.

I know it isn't always easy to be enthusiastic about a job which, for the time being, may be humdrum -- but I'll never forget the expression of pride and enthusiasm on the face of an old man who tended the boilers in a factory I visited recently.

Everything was brightly polished; every corner reflected his desire to put the best he had to give into his job.

"This is my baby," he said. And he looked as proud as though he'd been the chief engineer of the Queen Mary.

JUNE 28th

HOW TO INCREASE SALES

Rule 13: Good manners are good business -- for you, and for your company.

It pays, all down the line, not only to be pleasant but to feel kindly toward everyone.

Courtesy, like enthusiasm, also is contagious. It is reflected in the attitudes of everyone who is exposed to it.

One pleasant, smiling, courteous personality can change the atmosphere of an entire office or plant.

And, believe it or not, it helps increase sales.

JUNE 29th

HOW TO INCREASE SALES

Rule 14: Make the most of every working minute, for time is the most valuable possession you own.

On what you do with each day's time depends the direction in which you are heading in your company.

You own as much time as the richest man who ever lived. Don't lose any of it.

Make each moment count by putting more into it.

JUNE 30th
HOW TO INCREASE SALES

Rule 15: Keep things simple and you not only will save your own time, but the time of others in the company.

This advice applies to letters, conversations, phone calls, reports, conferences, meetings and every other business activity.

The employee who can simplify things is more valuable in any job.

JULY 1st
HOW TO INCREASE SALES

Rule 16: TRY to avoid making mistakes, but don't be AFRAID to make one occasionally.

The man who never made a mistake has never tried anything new.

Progress would cease tomorrow if everyone was afraid to risk making an occasional mistake.

JULY 2nd

HOW TO INCREASE SALES

Rule 17: Set a goal for yourself and concentrate on it. Make it a worthy goal -- not merely the making of money, but rather the thrill of accomplishment.

It is natural for anyone to want more money, but we have to remember that money is payment for service rendered. It follows the rendering of a service; it never precedes it.

If our goal is to render increasingly valuable service, we need not worry about the ultimate reward.

Increase your sales and the reward will be tendered, in increased income.

JULY 3rd

HOW TO INCREASE SALES

Rule 18: Look upon your job as an open road, not as a dead-end street, for opportunity is and always has been unlimited -- except to those who lack the readiness and willingness both to recognize and to grasp it.

Just think of the countless doors that have opened to new and undreamed of opportunities in the past few years.

Opportunity is as limitless as the mind of man. As long as we use our minds to think with, opportunity will continue to knock at our door.

JULY 4th

HOW TO INCREASE SALES

Rule 19: Like the fathers of our country honored on this Independence Day, welcome responsibility with open arms. Don't fear it; don't run away from it.

A man must swim against the tide to develop strong swimming muscles.

And, in our jobs, we must take on more and more responsibility in order to develop our "work muscles" and prove how big a work load we can carry.

The man who is afraid of responsibility is afraid to succeed, and his progress is limited until he overcomes his fear.

JULY 5th

HOW TO INCREASE SALES

Rule 20: Don't be a "juggler." Make it a habit to finish each thing you start, before starting another project.

Don't try to juggle four or five projects "in the air" at the same time. It is costly -- time consuming -- and nearly always leads to errors

Smiley Anders

JULY 6th

HOW TO INCREASE SALES

Rule 21: Learn the difference between the important and unimportant.

Always put the most important things first, despite the fact that it is human nature to put first on the list the things we like to do -- the easier things, the more pleasant things.

When you tackle the tough, important things first -- as you should -- you make the rest of the day's work all the easier.

JULY 7th

HOW TO INCREASE SALES

Rule 22: Think things through before you start -- then proceed confidently to execute them.

And, when you have a difficult assignment, figure it out for yourself first.

Then, and only then, should you ask someone else for advice.

JULY 8th

HOW TO INCREASE SALES

Rule 23: Be sure that you have the facts before making a decision.

Most mistakes are made by people who fail to take the trouble to get the facts before arriving at their conclusions.

JULY 9th

HOW TO INCREASE SALES

Rule 24: Initiate -- don't imitate.

It does not require much brain work to be an imitator; to be guided solely by the way in which someone else performs a given task.

Increase sales by your own ingenuity.

The other's method may or may not be the best -- for you, or for the company. There may be a better way. Use your imagination.

This is the way that new and better methods are developed. This is the way that more sales are made.

JULY 10th

HOW TO INCREASE SALES

Rule 25: Show clearly, in everything you do and say, that you have a genuine interest in your job and in the welfare of the company you work for.

Think of it, and speak of it, as "MY company" or "OUR company" -- not merely as "THE company."

For you are a part of it. Its success is your success, to the extent that you give more of your thought, your effort and your loyalty to make its success possible

JULY 11th

HOW TO INCREASE SALES

Rule 26: It will help you to keep reminding yourself that "Success never is an accident" -- it has to be earned through service.

Yes, each one of us must give more in order to get more in his job.

Success is the reward for accomplishment.

JULY 12th

NOT "GOOD ENOUGH"

Today "good enough" is not enough.

Only our best will pass the test in today's highly competitive economy.

Doesn't it stand to reason that the people who do get ahead, and the companies that get ahead, are those who strive for excellence?

Those who are trying continually to: do a better job; make a better product; render better service; improve their working relationships; attract more customers, and increase the quality and value in every possible way.

Just "good enough" is NOT enough.

JULY 13th

QUALITY COUNTS

That word "quality" is a mighty important one to remember.

In your company, or any company you can name, "quality" is everybody's responsibility.

This is why the individual who fails to rise to the challenge of excellence either in what he does (workmanship) or in what he is (character) has no right to expect more benefits, more pay or more consideration from his employer.

We can't accomplish much in our jobs unless we strive for excellence in everything we do, including our everyday relations with other people.

JULY 14th

NO STRINGS ATTACHED

When you pick up light summer reading, you expect it to be just that.

But the other day "September Child" by Jean Dalrymple chanced across my desk. She spent her early years with a governess-housekeeper, Miss High, whose wisdom was remembered long after she was no longer around. Snapping beans together when Jean was 5, Miss High held up a bean and said, "Don't leave any strings attached. Always work a little longer and a little harder and a little more carefully than the others around you.

You will never achieve perfection -- no one does --but try for it. Then you will be able to say to yourself and to the world, too, 'I did my best.'"

I think I shall long remember the simple illustration with the beans: "Don't leave any strings attached."

JULY 15th
A WORD ABOUT COOPERATION

It is only under extenuating circumstances that you are required to give a little extra of yourself, your time, your effort, in order to expedite a special service to a customer who has not given prior notice of his needs.

Occasionally your supervisor is not in a position to lend a hand in these situations due to previous commitments.

It is at rare times like these that a salesman has the opportunity to demonstrate his job interest and cooperative attitude.

Unselfish cooperation is important at all times.

JULY 16th
WELCOME THE MORNING

Someone wrote a book, "Life Begins at 40." I rise to offer a substitute title: "Life Begins Each Morning."

Take each day and use it as best you can. Or, if you prefer to waste it, that is your privilege (although it is unwise and unprofitable).

Each morning is the open door to a new world -- new vistas, new aims, new trying

JULY 17th
NEVER TOO LATE

The greatest fact of life is this; that it is never too late to start again.

History overflows with startling examples of this truth.

However discouraging your days may have been thus far, keep this thought burning brightly in your mind: Make the most of each day!

JULY 18th
HONESTY ON THE JOB, PART 1

It is an alarming fact that dishonesty in business is taking money out of the pockets of many hard-working, trustworthy employees, by cutting into the profits of the companies for which they work.

Business dishonesty can take many forms:

Not giving a full day's work for a full day's day is dishonest.

Loafing on the job, overstaying time in the restroom, stretching a lunch hour -- these are all minor forms of dishonesty.

JULY 19th

HONESTY ON THE JOB, PART 2

Dishonesty can wear many faces:

Unnecessary personal telephone calls; seeking special privileges, such as taking time off without a valid reason; "disowning" a mistake instead of owning up to it, are a few of the masks for business misconduct.

Chronic tardiness is still another way of cheating your employer.

JULY 20th

HONESTY ON THE JOB, PART 3

There are all types of destructive dishonesty in business relationships:

A falsely ambitious employee may withhold information about a new project, or a better way of performing a particular task, in hopes of later impressing his superior.

Facts may be withheld from fellow workers in order that one person may get all the credit.

On the other hand, if you are entrusted with confidential data about the company, then revealing such policies is a form of dishonesty.

JULY 21st

HONESTY ON THE JOB, PART 4

Is taking small amounts of time, or materials, or money, really so deplorable?

Is it a crime if a secretary takes home a package of typing paper because the kids can use it?

So what if a messenger takes two hours to make a delivery and "clocks in" four hours later?

Is the boss going to miss the handful of postage stamps the shipping clerk scoops up at the end of the day?

Does it matter if the bookkeeper "borrows" a dollar from petty cash and forgets to pay it back?

Dishonesty can't be measured in terms of size. Stealing is stealing, no matter how large or small the item taken.

JULY 22nd

HONESTY ON THE JOB, PART 5

Honesty can't be split up like a pie. A person can't be honest with his family and friends and dishonest with his employer and call himself an honest person.

It's time the good people in the world stopped being ashamed about being honest and became more vocal in their demands for a code of ethics in business, at home and in government.

Padding expense accounts and juggling tax records are no longer considered serious offenses by many people -- if they can get away with it.

Times may change -- but honesty never goes out of style.

JULY 23rd

HONESTY ON THE JOB, PART 6

"Everybody's doing it!" is no excuse or face-saving alibi. The fact is, everybody is NOT doing it -- if a responsible person has the coverage to say "No."

You know the kind of standards you want maintained in your own home. Can a person expect less from himself at work?

We cannot operate on a double standard of morality. We cannot preach honesty and respect at home, while defying it in business.

JULY 24th

HONESTY ON THE JOB, PART 7

Profits alone are no longer the sole criterion of the successful businessman.

Today's businessman takes an active part in his community. The businessman very often sets the tone of his community.

The man who wishes to succeed must be smart enough to seize a good bargain, and honest enough not to take advantage of anyone.

And this applies equally to employees

JULY 25th

HONESTY ON THE JOB, PART 8

An employee is an accessory to a crime if he is aware of dishonest activity and remains silent.

Silence is not golden -- it can be negligence, even criminal negligence.

"I don't want to get involved" or "I don't want to be a squealer" are not excuses.

JULY 26th

HONESTY ON THE JOB, PART 9

"Honesty is the best policy" for your own health and peace of mind.

Nothing can be as wearing on a person as gnawing guilt. It corrodes the spirit, the soul.

Dishonesty breeds fear. A dishonest employee is not a happy worker. He is always worried and on edge about who is watching him, and why.

Dishonesty drains a person emotionally and physically.

The honest person, on the other hand, has that priceless asset of self-respect. And the man who can respect himself will respect all others.

JULY 27th

HONESTY ON THE JOB, PART 10

It has been said that "Honesty is not only the first step toward greatness -- it is greatness itself."

Honesty also breeds confidence. The honest worker goes about his job more successfully and efficiently.

Customers are attracted to a company whose employees act in an open and above-board manner.

Investors are attracted to a company whose policies and procedures are revealed fully and frankly.

Big business cannot survive on little lies.

JULY 28th

LOVE STORY

"You say you love me but sometimes you don't show it.

"In the beginning, you couldn't do enough for me. Now you seem to take me for granted.

"Some days I even wonder if I mean anything at all to you...

"I'm responsible for getting the food on your table, for the clean shirt you wear every day, for the welfare of your children...

"Why, if it weren't for me you wouldn't even have a car to drive...

"Cherish me, take care of me and I'll continue to take good care of you.

"Who am I?

"I am your job."

JULY 29th

KNOW YOUR COMPETITION

Your competitor is leaving no stone unturned in his efforts to take your customers away from you.

Know the products of your competitors, know their selling methods, know as much as you can about them.

Call on some of your competitors' customers, and emphasize to them our advantages and methods of doing business.

Get on the ball; overcome your competitors' overtures to your customers with good service and a closer personal relationship with your customers.

JULY 30th

BOTTOM FEEDERS

If you've made up your mind that you prefer the bottom of the ladder, here are five ways to maintain your position:

1. Resist change. Don't march into the future -- back into it.

2. Plunge wildly into great schemes, forsaking all reason or judgment.

3. Squander your strength; burn the candle at both ends. Embrace motion without progress.

4. Eschew humanity. Be too tough for kindness, too cold for sympathy, too busy for friendship.

5. Play it safe. Never stick your neck out or take a chance.

JULY 31st

AT SET OF SUN

By S.L. Heine

If you sit down at set of sun

And count the acts that you have done,

And, counting, find

One self-denying deed, one word

That eased the heart of him who heard --

One glance most kind,

That fell like sunshine where it went --

Then you may count that day well spent.

But if, through all the live long day,

You've cheered no heart, by yea or nay --

If, though it all

You've done nothing that you can trace

That brought the sunshine to one face --

No act most small

That helped some soul and nothing cost --

Then count that day as worst than lost.

AUGUST 1st

FEAR FACTOR

Many sales executives will testify that fortunes are being lost because business and industry cannot find enough young men who are unafraid.

Smiley Anders

What seems strange about this picture is that business and industry are not bidding for trigger-happy or switch-blade bravado. On the contrary, business and industry bid for just enough simple courage to meet your fellow man on an equal footing and without fear.

Some old-timers in the selling business will confess that they, too, have a momentary period of "torture" just before they are to face up to a new prospect.

But they have learned how to bridle nervousness, to convert this energy into energy for the job to be done, and into a sale.

AUGUST 2nd

FEAR FACTOR, PART 2

Many public speakers admit they are "keyed up" before every speech they make. Once they are on their feet and they have begun to expound on their subject and jitters vanish.

So it can be with selling. The salesman who tries to run away from needless fear in licked.

AUGUST 3rd

FEAR FACTOR, PART 3

Knowledge of your produce or the service you sell will give you the self-assurance you need.

Just remember, you probably know more about the product or service you have to sell than your prospect does.

In other words, you are, or should be, a specialist on the subject

AUGUST 4th

FEAR FACTOR, PART 4

When you finally meet your prospect you'll probably discover no signs of the unpleasantness that you may have anticipated.

You are there to perform a service for your prospect. You are there to show him how he can make a profit by using what you have to sell. You are there to show your prospect how he (or she) can get more business, obtain certain pleasures, gain knowledge, health or other benefits by buying from you.

That is your mission. You are not an intruder. You are there to serve.

AUGUST 5th

FEAR FACTOR, PART 5

Until a method is devised to crack whatever it is that terrifies some new salesmen, just so long will the cost of building an effective sales force continue to climb.

The individual salesman's income will either sag or fail to rise to its potential.

There is little use laying all the blame to laziness, because a study of the situation reveals that in case after case fear -- fear or failure, fear of embarrassment, fear of meeting a belligerent prospect, fear of indefinable things -- is the monster behind the problem.

AUGUST 6th

FEAR FACTOR, PART 6

A survey of more than 100 successful sales executives in various lines revealed that simple stage fright is a common problem in bringing new salesmen across the first bridge to the big payoff.

But stage fright is something that can be overcome.

Almost anyone fired by enthusiasm; ambition and a desire to succeed can learn to think on his feet.

Self-confidence and poise can be developed, and these qualities will soon chase stage fright away.

This is the bridge of courage that most of us must cross to stack up a more impressive sales record.

AUGUST 7th

SPOKEN WORDS

Spoken words are keys to success. They can open doors and avenues which will help us to achieve.

And not unusual or grandiose words either. The spoken words which may fittingly be called keys to success are simple, ordinary, everyday words.

They are words learned in childhood, words of clear and unmistakable meaning. Yet they are hard to say at the right time and in the right way.

These words are "Please!", "Thank you!", "Yes!", "No!", "Goodbye!"

AUGUST 8th

SPOKEN WORDS: "Please"

When we say "Please," it demonstrates to those who hear it that we are not arrogant and demanding, that we recognize the dignity and equality of those of whom we make our request.

This is the key to pleasant social relationships.

We must not, however, use the word improperly. There is no magic in its mere utterance, and repetitious utterance actually decreases its door-opening power.

To be effective, "Please" must be spoken quietly and sincerely.

AUGUST 9th

SPOKEN WORDS: "Thank You"

"Thank you" is the key of appreciation, When we use it, we show to others that we are not too self-centered, too conceited to recognize service well performed.

People like to be appreciated; it is one of the deep-seated urges of the human soul.

It is not the biggest tippers who get the best service in our hotels and restaurants. It is, rather, those who by their words and their actions prove their appreciation.

Any successful salesman will attest to the validity of this statement.

"Thank you" is never out of place

AUGUST 10th

SPOKEN WORDS: "Yes"

"Yes" is the key of leadership. It opens the door to opportunity.

It demonstrates our ability to rise above the rut of everyday activities to accept the challenge of new and pattern-shattering ideas, duties, and responsibilities.

The man or woman who can say "Yes" to the right things and the right people is a man or woman marked in the eyes of the community as one destined for success.

"Will you serve on the board of your church?"

"Will you take this work home tonight so we can start shipping tomorrow morning?"

These are the kinds of questions to which "Yes" opens doors to success.

AUGUST 11th

SPOKEN WORDS: "No"

"No" is the key of character. It opens the door to personal influences.

The man or woman who has said "No" to the wrong things and the wrong people is known as a person who can be trusted, who has the courage of his or her convictions, who will not betray standards and values no matter how attractive the offers of personal gain.

It takes character and courage to say "No."

AUGUST 12th

SPOKEN WORDS: "Goodbye"

"Goodbye" is the key of reverence. The use of "Toodleloo," "Be seein' yah," "So long" and similar words of farewell cannot take its place.

They will not open the door; they connote no deep personal concern about the person from whom we depart or who departs from us.

It is also a prayer, the condensation of the sentence "God be with you."

AUGUST 13th

SALUTE TO COMPETITORS

This was found in an old issue of Progressive Grocer magazine:

"My competitors do more for me than my friends do; my friends are too polite to point out my weaknesses, but my competitors go to great expense to advertise them.

"My competitors force me to search for ways to improve my products and service.

"My competitors would take my business away from me if they could; this keeps me alert to hold what I have.

"If I had no competitors, I would be lazy, incompetent, inattentive; I need the discipline they enforce upon me."

AUGUST 14th

MAN'S SIX MISTAKES

From Cicero:

1. The delusion that individual advancement is made by crushing others.

2. The tendency to worry about things that cannot be changed or corrected.

3. Insisting that a thing is impossible because we cannot accomplish it.

4. Refusing to set aside trivial preferences.

5. Neglecting development and refinement of the mind, and not acquiring the habit of reading and study.

6. Attempting to compel other persons to believe and live as we do.

AUGUST 15th

THE AGING OF NATIONS

The average age of the world's greatest civilizations has been 200 years. These nations progressed through this sequence:

From bondage to spiritual faith.

From spiritual faith to great courage.

From courage to liberty.

From liberty to abundance.

From abundance to selfishness.

From selfishness to complacency.

From complacency to apathy.

From apathy to dependency.

From dependency back to bondage.

AUGUST 16th

THE PRICE OF FREEDOM

If an employee worked eight hours a day and did everything that the employer expected of him, then this man would be a slave to his job. But if this man did a little MORE than what was expected of him, came in a little earlier and left a little later, then he would be a free man.

He wouldn't have to ask to take an afternoon off to go to a ballgame or go fishing because he has paid the price of freedom, gone the extra mile, and he is a free man.

AUGUST 17th

A MILLION DOLLARS

I was at a meeting where the members were asked what we would do if someone gave us a million dollars.

I was amazed at the answers -- people were going for extended vacations, retiring to their favorite resort area, doing everything except what they do for a living.

I thought to myself, how miserable these people must be at their work.

I told them that I really believe with all my heart that if I had a million dollars I would continue to do the same thing I am doing now.

Just look around at the opportunity we have to serve people. Only by serving people can we achieve real rewards in life.

AUGUST 18th
JUST CHECKING

We should be like the little boy who walked into a drug store, put a coin in the phone, dialed a number and said, "Dr. Anderson, have you a yard boy? Oh, you have. Are you satisfied with him? Oh, you are. Well, thank you, Dr. Anderson."

As he started walking out the door, the druggist said, "Hey, come back here, I need a yard boy."

The youngster said, "I already have a job. I'm Dr. Anderson's yard boy. I was just checking up on myself."

AUGUST 19th
LISTEN TO BEN

Benjamin Franklin, in his autobiography, gave us some basic rules:

Plan for future conduct: Have a plan and follow it.

Endeavor to speak truth in every instance; aim at sincerity in every word and action.

Do not be diverted from your business by any foolish project of growing suddenly rich; for industry and patience are the surest means of plenty.

Resolve to speak ill of no man whatever.

AUGUST 20th

CAN YOU RUN A BUSINESS?

Every think about running your own company? Most people do, at one time or other.

Every year about 350,000 Americans go beyond the dreaming stage and put their ideas into action. Unfortunately, a huge percentage of these new companies fail.

Few men seem to cross the gap between dreaming about a company and running it well. Why is this?

A successful company has to do at least three things:

1. Win customers.

2. Keep its costs and prices in line with the competition.

3. Satisfy its stockholders.

AUGUST 21st

CAN YOU RUN A BUSINESS?

1.   Winning Customers.

You don't TELL the customer what he wants, you GIVE him what we wants.

In a free economy like ours, another company will always spring up to give the customer what he wants if his present supplier doesn't provide it.

The only guarantee of success in a free economy is customer satisfaction.

AUGUST 22nd

CAN YOU RUN A BUSINESS?

2.   Meeting the Competition

Competition falls into two categories -- price and quality.

You've heard the old saying that the world will beat a path to the door of the man who builds better mousetrap. This is not quite true. If your mousetrap happens to cost $5.95, most people will settle for a poorer one at 49 cents.

The ability to hold costs down in order to meet competition is vital.

But you must match your competitors in quality, or the sales go to them.

*Smiley Anders*

Close control of costs is the key to winning the competitive race.

AUGUST 23rd

CAN YOU RUN A BUSINESS?

3.   Satisfying the Stockholders

The cash every business requires to finance its operations must be bought and paid for, just like nuts, bolts and typewriters.

You can't put over a good product without spending money -- lots of it.

When the money comes from stockholders, the company has an obligation to put money in the investor's pocket. Many people fail to appreciate this.

AUGUST 24th

CAN YOU RUN A BUSINESS?

4.   What If You Don't?

You don't have to be in business for yourself to know the ingredients that go into running a successful company. The man or woman who knows these ingredients is automatically a more valuable employee.

You may never go into business for yourself. You probably value your peace of mind too much, plus your leisure hours and your family's security.

140

But nothing can stop you from adding to your current worth and security by following company policy and helping your boss with HIS problems!

AUGUST 25th

DO YOU QUALIFY?

The U.S. Department of Commerce put out a report in which the department summarized the qualifications of a good businessman. This applies equally to the employee.

Listed were leadership, ambition, initiative, energy and good health. But along with these traits, the Department of Commerce emphasized that the man who wishes to succeed must be "smart enough to seize a good bargain, and honest enough not to take advantage of anyone."

AUGUST 26th

POSITIVE THINKING

Your subconscious mind is a recording machine which faithfully reproduces whatever you impress upon it.

For example, you may be polite and courteous to someone in your office, but when his back is turned you are very critical and resentful toward him in your mind.

Such negative thoughts are highly destructive to you. Negative thoughts and emotions since down into your subconscious and cause all kinds of difficulties.

"Judge not, that ye not be judged." Matthew 7:12.

AUGUST 27th

HOW TO DISAGREE

If you have not done so already, you must learn to disagree without being disagreeable.

It is never what a person says or does that affects him; it is his reaction to what is said or done that matters.

There are salesmen who have difficulties in working with their sales manager and supervisor. They seem to think that the sales manager and supervisor do not like them, that they are unjustly treated, and at sales meetings the sales manager was rude to them or ridiculed their suggestions.

When you become emotionally mature, you do not respond negatively to the criticism of others.

AUGUST 28th

THE VALUE OF PEACE

Identify yourself with your aim in life, and do not permit any person, place or thing to deflect you from your inner sense of peace, tranquility and good health.

Do not permit people to take advantage of you and gain their point by temper tantrums, crying jags, etc.

These people are dictators who try to enslave you and make you do their bidding.

Be firm but kind, and refuse to yield. Appeasement never wins.

AUGUST 29th

THE RIGHT SLANT

If selling our products is the most interesting job you can imagine, you'll sell all right -- no doubt about it. But if you look upon the work you do as just another job, you'll get by, probably, but you'll never make the big success you want. Your slant will be wrong.

If you have the right slant now, fine. You're lucky.

If not, get it. Make up your mind today that there isn't anything more important in your life than our products.

Try that slant for a week, and if your sales aren't higher than during any week of your life, I'll miss my guess.

AUGUST 30th

LIVING TO SERVE

At the end of life, we shall not be asked how much pleasure we had in it, but how much service we gave to it; not how full it was of success, but how full it was of sacrifice; not how happy we were, but how helpful we were; not how ambition was gratified, but how love was served.

AUGUST 31st

LIVE FOR TODAY

As I got older I became aware of the folly of this perpetual reaching after the future and drawing from tomorrow and tomorrow only a reason for the joyfulness of today.

I learned almost too late to live each moment as it passed over my head.

SEPTEMBER 1st

THE VALUE OF THE SALESMAN

It's the salesman who keeps workers at their jobs. The efforts of the salesman are felt in areas he never suspected.

Selling is an art, a physical accomplishment and a mental conquest. It is not work for the week, nor is it a job for the irresponsible.

It is a proving ground for men who devote themselves to a profession and move ahead where others would faint and fail.

To be frank -- selling is a hard grind and deserving of a proper perspective.

SEPTEMBER 2nd

NOT "JUST A JOB"

If selling our products is the most interesting job you can imagine, you'll sell all right; no doubt about it.

But if you look upon the work you do as just another job, you'll get by, probably, but you'll never make the big success you want. Your slant will be wrong.

If you have the right slant now, fine. You're lucky. If not -- get it.

Just make up your mind that there isn't anything more important in your life than our products.

SEPTEMBER 3rd

SELL YOURSELF

Many times the sale and promotion of your product depend entirely on how well you, the salesman, has sold himself.

This does not mean how many times you have taken the store owner or manager to lunch or other social activities, but on the service you perform checking prices, rotation, inventory, etc.

The salesman should be a one-man service organization, bridging the gap between his company and the retailer.

SEPTEMBER 4th

IMPORTANT QUESTIONS

One of the best producers I know has a checklist that he goes over as soon as he gets back to his vehicle after an unproductive call. Here are some of the questions he asks himself:

Would the customer have benefited from the purchase?

What did he lose by not buying?

Did the man I called on have the power to buy?

Did I tell the customer or prospect the whole story, covering all points in the proper sequence, despite interruptions?

Did I speak in terms of benefits that meant something to him?

(Continued)

SEPTEMBER 5th

IMPORTANT QUESTIONS, PART 2

More questions a top producer asks himself after an unproductive call:

Did I have solid evidence -- third party, if possible -- to prove my claims?

Did I listen carefully when he talked?

Was I able to answer his questions without bluffing?

Did he present any major objection that I was unable to handle with finesse?

(Continued)

SEPTEMBER 6th

IMPORTANT QUESTIONS, PART 3

Final questions a top producer asks himself after an unproductive call:

Did I draw him out with questions?

Did I give up really trying to sell him the first time he said "No"?

Did I specifically ask him for an order?

How many times?

Did I have a good closing argument?

SEPTEMBER 7th

JOIN THE TEAM

The modern salesman believes in and practices complete cooperation with his employer.

He not only accepts supervision, but requests instruction and guidance.

He participates in his company's sales meetings, and does all he can to make such an event succeed.

He joined wholeheartedly in planned "drives," and pulls his weight in contests.

Today, each person must be an active member of "the team" or make room for someone else who will join willingly and sincerely in the common effort to increase sales

SEPTEMBER 8th

KEEP THE CIGARS

The day of the salesman who went around handing out expensive cigars, slapping people in the back, entertaining lavishly and telling a new crop of stories on each visit is definitely gone.

Buyers are required by today's competitive conditions as well as by a change in ethical standards to treat the social as subordinate to the business components of their transactions.

The sales interview is no longer a time of persuasion by spell-binding. It has become instead of time of persuasion by education.

Facts have replaced jokes; information is now preferred to cigars.

SEPTEMBER 9th

THE OTHER SIDE

Competition is the motivating force of the private enterprise system, but it is neither as ruthless nor as uncivilized as it was a few decades ago.

In fact, competitors in most industries cooperate through their trade associations to promote the interest of everyone engaged in the industry.

When you meet a competitor, be aloof without being unfriendly. That attitude will reflect your conviction that your product is as good as, or better than, the product of the competitor.

SEPTEMBER 10th

THE PROFESSIONAL BUYER

Buying has become more professional. Today, buyers are subject to greater management control than ever before; more than ever they must "buy right."

They look to the salesman to aid them in their task.

To execute his proper function, the salesman must be equipped with fact, statistics and knowledge of various sorts that would surprise his predecessor of only a few decades ago.

The salesman must always have sufficient technical knowledge to give the prospect the information he wants and needs.

SEPTEMBER 11th

THE PAPER CHASE

The salesman who is loath to fill out required reports must be reminded that the day is gone in which the salesman can say, "Oh, hang the paper work!

As long as I'm out there pitching hard and writing up orders, everything will be OK!"

Such a man is out of step with the realities of modern salesmanship.

Do your paper work during non-selling hours.

SEPTEMBER 12th

A MATTER OF CONFIDENCE

Very possibly the salesman will make little specific use of the product data drilled into him when he gets down to actual selling.

Just as you seldom go around reciting the multiplication table or quoting any Latin verse you may have learned in school, so he will probably never have cause to mention to a customer the various facts he has absorbed.

But the fact that he knows them will get across. It will give him confidence in himself; it will give him the easy assurance that comes with being able to handle any questions or doubtful points that may arise; it will enable him to convince a customer that he really knows what he is talking about.

SEPTEMBER 13th

THE OLD AND THE NEW

Are you selling yesterday's customers or today's customers?

There's a big difference; concentration on the former means a dead halt to sales increases for any salesman.

The big commission builders are always the new customers whose needs are greater in most cases.

Coupling close attention to good salesmanship with one's old customers and an all-out drive to secure new customers can invariably build a lagging sales figure for the salesman.

SEPTEMBER 14th

COMPLAINT DEPARTMENT

A leader should settle all grievances, if possible. The unsettled complaint of one worker affects everyone.

If one person gripes, find out why. His gripe may be the gripe of many.

Criticize constructively. Give reasons for criticisms and ways to correct them. Precede criticisms with good points; let the employee know you want to help him.

If a worker's behavior seems unusual, find out why.

Whether you are a "boss" or a "leader" can make the big difference in your relationship with employees.

SEPTEMBER 15th

HOW TO THANK A CUSTOMER

"Thank you for sending business our way. There's nothing we like to go more than say 'thanks' to you, our customer.

"We hope you never find us guilty of failing to express our appreciation for your orders.

"We know that you are responsible for keeping us in business.

"That's why we like saying to you -- thanks."

SEPTEMBER 16th

THE WEEDING-OUT PROCESS

Getting rid of the non-performer puts a burden on sales managers.

It seems easier to keep on a man who is just barely adequate than to recruit and train a new man.

This practice is often defended as "costing us nothing." After all, it is argued, we pay a salesman commission only on what he sells.

But this is a delusion. Support costs are always there, and there is a much higher cost than his pay: the cost of missing sales.

There is nothing more expensive to a business than missed opportunities.

SEPTEMBER 17th

OBJECTION OVERRULED

"No man," said Carter D. Poland, successful businessman, "can call himself a salesman until he can muster two good reasons why the customer should buy from him for every one reason the customer can find why he shouldn't."

There's a saying among sales executives that a sale only starts when the customer says no.

SEPTEMBER 18th

THE PRICE IS RIGHT

One big and persistent snag which salesmen run into is the matter of price.

Many salesmen believe that price is the all-in-all of selling. They're more price-minded than their customers.

But Dr. George Gallup, conducting a nationwide survey, discovered that, in the vast majority of instances, price is not the first consideration, either with men or women, in making purchases.

Both consider other things first, price second.

(Continued)

SEPTEMBER 19th

THE PRICE IS RIGHT, PART 2

Years ago a business genius by the name of Lorin H. Deland made a discovery about price that should influence every salesman:

He discovered that price by itself is nothing at all; that the REASON for the price is the important thing in making a sale.

Any salesman who keeps this fact in mind won't have much difficulty in slaying the price bugaboo.

(Continued)

SEPTEMBER 20th

THE PRICE IS RIGHT, PART 3

In treating the matter of price, there are a new "don'ts" to keep in mind:

Don't get excited when the customer tells you your price is clear out of line. He may be just testing you.

Don't be afraid to talk back to the buyer who tells you to "sharpen your pencil." Tell him you don't do business that way.

Don't open a sales presentation on price; start off with more important factors.

Don't get into an argument about price.

Don't mention price before the prospect does; sell him on quality and service.

SEPTEMBER 21st

LIFE AND ITS CHANGES

Life has been described as a series of compulsory adjustments.

Changes come in every life; unasked for, unexpected.

How we face them -- with bitterness, resentment, or courage -- is the test.

Prayer helps. Through it we learn to accept life as it is, and not only to make the best of it but to make the MOST of it.

SEPTEMBER 22nd

THE WONDERS OF FRIENDSHIP

Some people choose their friends deliberately and with an ultimate goal in mind.

They select each one carefully, thinking only of the help and prestige which possibly will follow from such a relationship.

How different is the friendship which is unplanned, unexpected, uninhibited and often almost unexplainable!

It is as welcome to everyday living as a sudden burst of sunshine is to a dull gloomy day. It warms and mellows the heart, and helps us carry the responsibilities of life with a little less worry and fear.

SEPTEMBER 23rd

FIGHTING DISCOURAGEMENT

No one ever becomes so great that he doesn't time and again get discouraged.

In every walk of life we meet with discouragement, but it can be managed.

For one thing, it doesn't last forever. It's temporary, like losing something that can be replaced in time.

A little encouragement goes a long way. There is no medicine more potent for discouragement than that of giving out a little encouragement and appreciation, for these have medical power greater than any drug.

SEPTEMBER 24th
RANDOM THOUGHTS

Act as though it were impossible to fail.

Emulate: don't envy.

It is magnificent to grow old, if one keeps young.

The shadows of evening lengthen about me, but morning is in my heart.

Knowledge is what one knows; wisdom is knowledge and good judgment based on experience.

The men who try to do something and fail are infinitely better than those who try to do nothing and succeed.

SEPTEMBER 25th
MORE RANDOM THOUGHTS

There are no hopeless situations, there are only men who have grown hopeless about them.

The graveyards are full of people the world could not do without.

Before you can become a leader, you must learn to be a follower.

Success lies not in achieving what you aim at, but in aiming at what you ought to achieve and pushing forward, sure of achievement here; or if not here, hereafter.

Be aware of the thorns, but concentrate on the rose

SEPTEMBER 26th

THE ROYAL TREATMENT

The first time I went out with our senior salesman, he had me load the sales material in the car, do all the driving, put up sales displays, and even open and shut the car door for him. Finally I worked up enough courage to tell him what I thought of him.

"You've got a royalty complex," I said. "You expect me to wait on you hand and foot and act like I enjoy it! I went out with you to learn how to sell, remember?"

"You're learning," he said with a smile.

"Learning what?" I demanded. "All I've learned is how to treat you like a king."

"You're learning," he said, "how to treat customers."

SEPTEMBER 27th

TIME IS MONEY

There are 1952 working hours in a year of 244 working days.

To calculate the money value of your time, decide how much you want to earn in a year and divide your earnings goal by 1952 hours.

Now that you know how much each hour of your time is work, you can see the importance of using your time most judiciously.

You will agree that the most profitable hours are those you spent in actual selling or telling the story of your product.

Spend your time wisely and the rewards will be great.

SEPTEMBER 28th

THE VALUE OF DISCONTENT

If a man is contented and satisfied with what he calls his share of the business, it means he is too easily satisfied and is not an asset to his company.

It is only when a man is NEVER satisfied that he can succeed as a salesman.

If every salesman wanted his share, no more, there'd be no progress, no prosperity, no profit and no company for very long.

SEPTEMBER 29th

KNOW YOUR COMPETITION

A large tool manufacturer lost $3 million in sales one year because a competitor's new product made an entire segment of the tool company's line completely obsolete.

As the sales vice president of the company later said, "The worst of it is that we could and should have known of the development. Had we known we would have expanded our own product development efforts and brought out our new product much sooner."

More sales and profits have been lost because of a lack of up-to-date information than because of poor judgment

SEPTEMBER 30th

BACK TO BASICS

In executive offices all over America, campaigns are being devised to put zip into sales promotions, to pinpoint advertising, to improve marketing methods, to excite and sharpen salespeople.

The emphasis is on a return to fundamentals: be optimistic, enthusiastic and helpful, especially in providing service.

Above all, be informed, for the majority of consumers today are as knowledgeable as purchasing agents. They want facts rather than opinions.

OCTOBER 1st

YOUR PRICE IS RIGHT

Until you conquer your fear of "price competition" you will never be a successful salesman.

There is always a market for a fine car -- and one for jalopies.

It is up to you to convince your customer or prospect that you don't sell jalopies.

The Tiffany salesman does not worry because some "jewels" are sold for as little as a dime.

He concentrates on a sales talk other than price.

OCTOBER 2nd

MAKING THE BREAKS

You make your own breaks.

Business is waiting for you. The gold in the ground will not jump into your pockets. You have to get down, dig for it, and pick it up. You will be well paid for your effort.

The more often you expose yourself to prospects, the more sales you will make.

Luck does not make a successful salesman, a successful salesman makes his own luck.

OCTOBER 3rd

A FRESH LOOK

The value of looking at things from a different perspective is shown by this story:

The movie actress Pauline Fredericks was touring a tire plant for publicity photos. As she watched a tire being constructed, she said, "I don't see why those fellows insist on doing it the hard way. Every time a man finishes his part of the job he gets up and lugs the heavy tire over to someone else to finish it. If he had a little trolley with a hook on it like we have on some of the movie sets, he could slide it over to him without ever getting off his stool."

The tire builder agreed with her, and the trolleys were promptly installed.

OCTOBER 4th

OLD PRODUCT, NEW MARKET

The old-time carnival "pitch man" would take a 50-cent bar of Castile soap, but it into 36 one-inch cubs, wrap the cubes in tin foil then put them in envelopes with printed instructions extolling the merits of the miracle spot remover.

When used without water, the soap actually would remove most of the household stains on the fabrics of that era.

The manufacturer of the soap could have put out the same product in stick form and legitimately sold it for the same purpose.

But a lack of imagination allowed the pitch man to make the 1,700 percent profit.

OCTOBER 5th

JUST THE FACTS

A salesman named Dave Bell was confronted by companies served by a competitor who had told previous salesmen from his company that they were satisfied with the service and had no intention of switching.

Dave investigated the services the competitor offered. Then he made a list, and called on the prospects again.

"On this sheet of paper," he will tell a prospect, "I have listed all the help you get from our competitor. But over here on the left I have listed those things that WE do for you which you cannot get elsewhere."

Because the facts were on his side, and were presented in so clear a manner, he made sale after sale.

OCTOBER 6th

SIMPLE BUT EFFECTIVE

A salesman for Royal Cup Coffee Co. of Birmingham, Ala., was sent to Montgomery, Ala., where Royal Cup did not have a single account.

During the noon hour, he would have his soup in one restaurant, his main course in a second, and his dessert and coffee in a third. He would praise the food and get into a friendly talk with the owner or manager. He would offer to make an analysis of the restaurant's beverage sales, and in short order made a few sales.

Within little more than a year, eight restaurants, two hospitals, two homes for the aged and one large cafeteria were using Royal Cup's coffee and tea.

OCTOBER 7th

THE THEATER OF SALES

Often, effective communications can benefit from a sense of the theatrical. During World War II, Gen. Douglas MacArthur's statement "I shall return" was not only confidence-building, it was tremendously effective, persuasive communication.

It had a theatrical impact, just as did Winston Churchhill's call for "blood, sweat, and tears."

Logic and reason may be enough to do the job of convincing, but most sales leaders put something extra into their communications to be certain of persuading their audience.

OCTOBER 8th

FAIR WEATHER SALESMEN

There just isn't any room in selling for "Fair Weather Salesmen."

You know the kind: on top of the world when orders come easy, but "low as a snake's belly in a wagon rut" when the going gets tough a few days running.

They belong in the same category as the golfers who cuss their caddies, break their clubs and act like spoiled brats whenever they have a couple of bad shots in a row.

You can't win every day, at golf, poker, bridge or selling.

OCTOBER 9th

DECEIVING YOURSELF

We rationalize to keep from facing the truth about our failures.

A vice president of a company who was a former alcoholic described his behavior:

"When I was young and just out of college, I found the nicest people in bars. As I got older, I found the crowd deteriorating; the most charming people never showed any more.

"I couldn't believe I was becoming an alcoholic, so I figured out that the bartenders were responsible. They weren't as intelligent as they used to be when I was younger.

"So I moved from bar to bar. I felt certain that if bartenders were more interesting and informed, then all the best people would return."

OCTOBER 10th

BARRIERS TO SUCCESS

Dr. Burleigh B. Gardner, social anthropologist, has pointed out some of the reasons why supervisors and managers fail in spite of their conscious desire to succeed:

Desire to be something else.

Inability to make room for others.

Resistance to authority.

Basically these defenses, as seen at home and on the job, are attempts to maintain a sense of person worth. Unfortunately, they sometimes block our objective understanding of ourselves

OCTOBER 11th

ABOUT FEAR

The beginning salesman fears making his first call.

Fear plays no favorites; it comes to all men.

The champion fighter overcomes his closest contender because the contender is paralyzed with fright. Then the champ leaves his class and takes on the champ in a heavier class and is so stricken with fear he can barely lift his arms.

You have to face fear, wrestle with it, take it apart and tear it to pieces if you can.And you can if you want to.

OCTOBER 12th

ABOUT PERFECTION

Whatever you do with your life, and however hard and long you work at your self-improvement, know this for sure: You will never be a perfect man.

But you can always make more headway at trying to develop the abilities and good qualities you already possess than in entirely eliminating your bad habits and weaknesses.

Your faults and good points will probably always be with you. Decide to cash in on your good points and give the right-of-way to the things you know you can do well.

OCTOBER 13th

MORE THAN SELLING

In order to make a success in the selling profession today, you must concentrate on improving yourself in merchandising, store layout, shelf arrangement, selling your full line, good public relations, keeping credit accounts current, and passing on helpful ideas to customers to increase their overall business.

Customers are always willing to listen to good sales-increasing ideas, and they usually show their appreciation by featuring your product.

OCTOBER 14th

KNOW YOUR PRODUCT

Many salesmen struggle along without ever putting to use the most valuable sales assistant they have -- the manufacturer of the very product they are selling.

Your company provides you with a product designed and tested not only to stand up against competition but of fill specific wants of a large number of potential customers.

It pays to know everything there is to know about that product.

OCTOBER 15th

EXPRESS YOUR IDEAS

When you have ideas about the product you are selling, or thoughts on how sales can be made easier, by all means express them to management.

They may fit in with other ideas now in process, and may add up to something new which will provide you with a better product to sell more profitably.

Every manufacturer welcomes ideas; wise is the salesman who expresses them whenever the opportunity arrives.

OCTOBER 16th

TAKING STOCK

Inventory time for salesmen involves asking questions:

Did I put forth the necessary effort each day?

Did I take full advantage of the sales promotions put on by my company?

Have I put in a few extra hours each week seeking out new business?

What kind of public relations job have I done; do I get along well with my customers?

OCTOBER 17th

THE VALUE OF KNOWLEDGE

Practically everyone in sales now agrees that selling is a profession, and is changing rapidly. In order to keep up with the times, a salesman must do a great deal of studying.

A survey of the Sales Executive Club of New York found that 89% of those polled said past experience in a technical or non-selling field was valuable to increase general knowledge.

Almost all said constant reading and study were vital to success.

OCTOBER 18th

THE DEMAND FOR TRAINING

A survey of the Sales Executive Club of New York found that salesmen want more training from their own companies.

Some 60 percent of those surveyed felt they needed training in such general sales areas as sales psychology, personality development, customer service and basic techniques such as prospecting, closing, etc.

And 40 percent felt that their most important need was better knowledge of their products

OCTOBER 19th

HOW GOOD ARE YOU?

Answer in your own mind the following:

How good are you in price negotiations?

Do you see to it that the personnel of your customers are advised in selling your product?

Do you maintain adequate stocks and effective distribution?

How adequate are your follow-ups on new and prospective customers?

Do you furnish complete information with each new credit order?

Do you keep your division manager informed of the activities in your territory?

OCTOBER 20th

KNOW YOURSELF

Ask yourself these questions:

How much technical knowledge have you gained through education? Through self-development and experience?

How well do you know your own product?

How well do you know related products?

How well do you know pricing procedures and policies?

How well do you know the company, its objectives, organization and management philosophy?

How well do you know this business -- its economic, social and management philosophy?

OCTOBER 21st

A PERSONAL QUIZ

Ask yourself these questions:

Does your appearance appeal to customers?

Do you have annoying habits?

Can and do you keep a confidence?

Do you have courage to speak your mind against opposition?

Can you think under pressure or in front of a customer?

Do you explore all factors that might influence an order?

Are you determined to succeed?

Will you accept and use constructive criticism?

Do you enjoy the competitive side of selling?

OCTOBER 22nd

ASK YOURSELF

More questions for you to answer:

Do you act on your own initiative?

Do you originate new ideas and methods?

Do you do more than is required?

Do you seek out responsibility?

Do you put in a full day's work?

Do you spend your own time in self-improvement?

OCTOBER 23rd

YOU AND OTHERS

Ask yourself these questions:

Do you see your own responsibility and relationship with others in the organization?

Do you recognize your responsibilities for good relations with customers, suppliers and the public?

Are you generally respected by your associates?

Are you active in community affairs?

Are you active in trade associations?

Do you express yourself well?

Can you argue without being antagonistic?

Smiley Anders

OCTOBER 24th
THE BEST MEDICINE

Stop thinking about yourself. Lighten your own load by doing something for someone else.

It will keep you from morbid worry and fear. It's the best medicine.

There is only one way to happiness, and that is to cease worrying about things which are beyond our will.

Be not simply good; be good for something.

Those who want much are always much in need.

OCTOBER 25th
AVOID COMPLACENCY

Webster's definition of complacency: Pleased, contentment, smugness, self-satisfaction.

S.L. Heine's definition: Easy way, lack of interest, no ambition, lead poisoning (not in the blood stream).

Statistics prove that more businesses fail from the sin of complacency than any other reason.

When a company or a salesman become satisfied with the results of his efforts, he is signing his own business death warrant.

OCTOBER 26th

A SIMPLE ANSWER

One of the old-time salesmen I had the pleasure of knowing told me one day when I asked him how he consistently tripled his sales quota:

"See the people.

"Apply your product to your people's needs.

"Tell its story.

"Close the sale."

OCTOBER 27th

CATCH THAT RABBIT

There was a recipe for rabbit pie in an old English cookbook that started,

"First, catch the rabbit."

The recipe for salesmanship has just as plain a first step,

"First, find a customer."

The only way to catch a rabbit is to get out into the field.

The only way to find a customer is to get out and make calls, then make more calls.

OCTOBER 28th

THE 10 COMANDMENTS OF SUCCESS

No. 1 through No. 9

"Work like hell."

No. 10

"Keep on working like hell."

OCTOBER 29th

BENJAMIN'S WAY

In Benjamin Franklin's autobiography, he made this resolutions to improve himself:

He resolved:

1. To be frugal until I pay what I owe.

2. To endeavor to speak truth in every instance.

3. To apply myself industriously to whatever business I take in hand.

4. To speak ill of no man whatever.

OCTOBER 30th

RANDOM THOUGHTS

I once opened a meeting like this:

"This sales meeting will now come to order -- to see if we can get our customers to do likewise."

We can all profit by mistakes -- particularly if our competition makes enough of them.

To be 45 years young is sometimes far more cheerful and hopeful than to be 40 years old.

"He felt that he was growing old,

His nerves seemed very tense.

When he found a greener pasture,

He couldn't climb over the fence."

OCTOBER 31st

FEAR FACTOR

Halloween isn't the only time for being frightened.

Many sales executives will testify that fortunes are being lost because business and industry cannot find enough young men who are unafraid.

A survey of more than 100 successful sales executives in various lines revealed that simple stage fright is a common problem in bringing new salesman across the first bridge to the big payoff.

But stage fright can be overcome, by enthusiasm, ambition and a desire to succeed.

Self-confidence and poise can be developed, and these qualities will soon chase stage fright away.

NOVEMBER 1st

THE SPOKEN WORD

Spoken words are keys to success -- they can open doors and help us achieve our goals.

But they can also close doors and prevent us from achieving our goals.

The words that are the keys to success are simple, ordinary, everyday words: Please, thank you, yes, no and goodbye.

Used properly, they can help you realize your fondest hopes, dreams and aspirations

NOVEMBER 2nd

SAY PLEASE

The word "please" expresses humility and shows those who hear it that we are not arrogant and demanding, that we recognize the dignity and equality of those of whom we make our request.

This is the key to pleasant social relationships. It makes us pleasant to have around, nice to be with and agreeable to work for.

NOVEMBER 3rd

THE VALUE OF THANKS

"Thank you" shows appreciation -- when we use it, we show to others that we are not too self-centered, two conceited to recognize service well performed.

It can open the door to the respect and affection of others.

People like to be appreciated; it is one of the deep-seated urges of the human soul.

Any successful salesman can tell you that "thank you" is never out of place.

NOVEMBER 4th

ACCENT THE AFFIRMATIVE

"Yes" shows that we can rise to accept the challenge of new ideas, duties and responsibilities.

The man or woman who can say "yes" to the right things and the right people is a man or woman destined for success.

"Will you serve on the United Fund drive?"

"Will you take this work home with you tonight so we can start shipping in the morning?"

"Joe's wife is having a serious operation. Can you delay your vacation a day or so and take over his work so he can be with her?"

There are the kinds of questions to which "yes" opens the door to success.

NOVEMBER 5th

WHEN NEGATIVES ARE POSITIVE

Saying "no" can be the key to character. The man or woman who has said "no" to the wrong things and the wrong people is known as a person who can be trusted, who has the courage of his or her convictions and will not betray standards and values no matter how attractive the offers of personal gain.

It takes character and courage to say "no."

NOVEMBER 6th

LAST WORDS

Think of the word "good-bye" as a prayer, the condensation of the sentence "God be with you."

Used in this sense, "good-bye" can show that we are aware of a power greater than ourselves, and that we are deeply enough concerned for the welfare of our friend to ask the presence of that power with him wherever he goes

NOVEMBER 7th

THE CUSTOMER IS ALWAYS RIGHT

You don't TELL the customer what he wants, you GIVE him what he wants.

And it's not just the small outfits that must heed their customers' wishes. Big companies aren't above such things.

In a free economy like ours, new companies will always spring up to give the customer what he wants if his present supplier doesn't provide it.

Every company in the country, if it wants to stay in business, has to do the same thing.

NOVEMBER 8th

PRICE AND QUALITY

Competition falls into two categories: price and quality.

You must match your competitors in quality, or the sales go to them.

The greatest cause of most failures is that the companies cannot keep their costs in line with sales.

The ability to hold costs down in order to meet competition is a priceless ingredient.

NOVEMBER 9th

DON'T THINK NEGATIVE

The salesman's job is to change a prospect's reasons for not buying into reasons for buying; to help the prospect make a decision.

Often salesman actually solicits negative answers at the start of the presentation.

"I don't suppose you want to buy anything today, do you?"

Few salesmen would be inept enough to use these exact words, but their manner or facial expression will suggest them

NOVEMBER 10th

HOW TO SELL

The salesman's main purpose should be to tell his story as clearly, effectively, honestly and briefly as possible.

A well-organized selling format can grasp the customer's mind and carry it along without giving the prospect a chance to think of opposing ideas.

It is a psychological truth that no mind is brilliant enough to think of two things at once.

So if the salesman is presenting the reasons for buying effectively, he is then in control of the selling situation.

NOVEMBER 11th

THOSE NEGATIVE IDEAS

Many salesmen spent too much time on the negative side, trying to argue away the ideas opposed to buying instead of presenting the benefits and the reasons for buying.

It is impossible to talk persuasively enough to do away with these ideas opposed, and you don't have to.

They will come up as objections as the sale progresses, and even though you have a good offsetting answer they still remain when the customer mentally sums up and makes the decision

NOVEMBER 12th

HOW TO HEAR "YES"

When the salesman does a good job of telling his story with an organized selling plan, he has an excellent chance to getting a yes answer.

In a studied decision or even in impulse buying the mind of the customer goes through this process of contrasting the ideas opposed against the reasons for.

This is an excellent sales tool for controlling the closing part of the sale and to help the customer to say "yes."

NOVEMBER 13th

MAKING DECISIONS

Why is it so important for the salesman to always keep in mind that it is his main job to help the prospect make the decision?

No one likes to make decisions.

Making a decision means change -- we expose ourselves to risk and we hesitate and resist changing the existing condition.

Thank of the last time you were out on a vacation trip with your family and tried to decide where to stop for lunch

NOVEMBER 14th

HELPING THE CUSTOMER DECIDE

You can call on customers every day who are rocking along all right.

They may be miserable without your product or services and don't know it.

But, if you present your proposition and don't follow through by sticking with the prospect until he makes a decision, you may be doing him a greater disservice than never to have called on him in the first place.

NOVEMBER 15th
SUCCESSFUL SELLING TIPS, 1

Here are some suggested actions to help you step up your effectiveness as a salesman or saleswoman:

Learn at least three reasons why a prospect needs your product, three reasons why your product fits the need, three reasons why your product is a better buy than those sold by competitors, and three reasons why the prospect should buy now rather than later.

Study carefully all company literature concerning your products. Be sold on what you sell.

NOVEMBER 16th
SUCCESSFUL SELLING TIPS, 2

Watch your health.

Visit your doctor for a checkup periodically -- there is a relationship between your health and your attitude and your effectiveness as a salesman.

Don't talk to customers about your aches and pains, if you have them.

They usually are not interested

NOVEMBER 17th

SUCCESSFUL SELLING TIPS, 3

Be sincere. Learn what you need to know and don't bluff.

If you don't know, say so, but offer to find out.

Obtain proof to make the unbelievable believable to a buyer.

Whatever you do, don't make statements which you cannot back up; and above all, don't make promises you are unable to keep.

NOVEMBER 18th

SUCCESSFUL SELLING TIPS, 4

In selling you will be most successful when you follow the idea you are walking a tight rope.

Never give the impression that you are high-pressure, nor, on the other hand that you are indifferent.

Be properly dressed, not overdressed or underdressed.

Be friendly, not so friendly that you are considered familiar.

Don't be afraid to smile.

NOVEMBER 19th

SUCCESSFUL SELLING TIPS, 5

Put your merchandise in the hands of the prospect.

Get him to feel, smell or taste the difference when it is appropriate.

Give prospects, particularly those who might be skeptical, a chance to read selected printed material you have on any of your products.

Never knock competition. Concentrate on the value of your product relative to the price.

NOVEMBER 20th

SUCCESSFUL SELLING TIPS, 6

Ask for the order. Too many salesman do a real good job of making a sales presentation and then never realize the payoff, because they are reluctant to ask a prospect to buy.

Make the prospect's decision to buy easy, with a direct question such as, "How many do you wish to purchase?" or "May I write up your order now?"

NOVEMBER 21st

SUCCESSFUL SELLING TIPS, 7

A salesman or saleswomen should continually practice to improve his or her persuasion effectiveness.

I suggest you begin by thinking less about yourself and more about what the prospect you will be calling on wants and doesn't want, likes and doesn't like, and will do or will not do.

Then, make your presentation in terms of each prospect's problems, likes, dislikes and wants.

NOVEMBER 22nd

ADVICE TO OWNERS, 1

If you are the owner of a business employing a number of salesmen, the first thing you must decide is whether you are going to manage the salesmen yourself or hire a sales manager.

This is obvious, of course, but all too often owners who hire or appoint sales managers forget what the word "manager" means and keep their managers on strings, never delegating to them the authority they need to really do their jobs.

NOVEMBER 23rd

ADVICE TO OWNERS, 2

As owner of a business, you have to organize a first-string team. To recruit the men you want for such a team, you'll generally have to pay better than average wages.

Next you must organize this team and delegate authority.

Working behind the scenes with only your key personnel, you must give them full authority to do their jobs

NOVEMBER 24th

ADVICE TO OWNERS, 3

If your top management can't get results, replace them.

Your concern is only top level. You set the overall policy, tell your key personnel what you want and let them take over from there.

It is their responsibility to eliminate the misfits and incompetents from their areas until each department is running smoothly

NOVEMBER 25th

ADVICE TO OWNERS, 4

Once you have appointed your sales manager and other key personnel and given them the authority they need -- or better still, more than they need -- let THEM carry the ball and judge by the results.

After you have appointed your top level personnel, you should communicate only with them and not try to buypass them and deal with their subordinates.

If you see something being done wrong by a salesman, say nothing to the man doing it. Instead tell your sales manager and let him handle the situation.

NOVEMBER 26th

ADVICE TO OWNERS, 5

One thing to keep in mind is that there will always be times when you'll have to call on your top personnel to undertake difficult emergency jobs or to work unusually long hours.

It is in times like this that the respect, consideration and praise you have given them will pay off.

NOVEMBER 27th

ADVICE TO OWNERS, 6

Today we seem to be getting away from complimenting people on a job well done or rewarding them for a good suggestion.

Too often management is inclined to accept suggestions as its due and then claim credit for them itself.

Nothing kills employee initiative quicker.

Recognition plus a suitable raise is the quickest way to create a dedicated employee Dedicated employees are something every business needs almost as much as customers. They're like a magnet that draws in more customers.

NOVEMBER 28th

TAKING ORDERS

In today's economy, consumer reluctance very likely will test the wits of American salesmanship.

Order takers will be in real trouble.

Prosperity in the past has permitted sales forces to become less aggressive and dull, too satisfied to compete for new business, too placid to innovate.

Sales executives aren't going to tolerate these conditions much longer, nor can they, for the pressure is on them.

NOVEMBER 29th

SELLING WITH ZIP

In executive offices all over America, campaigns are being devised to put zip into sales promotions, to pinpoint advertising, to improve marketing methods, to excite and sharper sales people.

The emphasis is on a return to fundamentals: be optimistic, enthusiastic and helpful, especially in providing service. Above all, be informed, for the majority of consumers today are as knowledgeable as purchasing agents. They want facts rather than opinions

NOVEMBER 30th

THE NEED FOR SUPPORT

Most sales executives concede that the world's finest salesman can do little with a poor product or if his company does not support him with instruction, promotional materials and customer service.

Some salesmen are poor producers not because they lack talent but because they are improperly supervised.

All too often, when a new salesman is hired the supervisor tends to leave that salesman to his own devices. Salesmen must have intelligent supervision and coaching.

DECEMBER 1st

YOU HAVE TO TELL THEM

For heaven's sake, don't make your customers guess what you have to sell --

tell them, tell them, not once but as many times as necessary for them to know what a complete line you have to serve them with.

One of our salesmen had been calling on a customer for five years when the customer learned accidentally, of an addition to our line.

The salesman hadn't told him, but when he found out about it, he immediately put in an order and has been buying ever since.

DECEMBER 2nd

THE SHORT TERM

You must differentiate long-range personal goals from short-range ones.

Short-range goals are defined as:

Learning a little more about my job; making small improvements in performance, analyzing current security and methods for improvements.

These areas are immediate and 75 percent capable of achievement.

Long-range goals are vague and indefinite, like lots of money, prestige, becoming president, retirement, freedom from demands.

The problem for most people lies in the fact that people dream of making changes to achieve long-range goals which water down the energy to make oneself a little better tomorrow

DECEMBER 3rd

BACK AT THE OFFICE

Listen to a group of salesmen standing around in the evening swapping yarns, and 9 times out of 10 one of them will sooner or later relate the time-honored story of "How I got the office told off."

There are times when you get a letter or memo from someone in the office that gets under your skin -- "Where does that so-and-so get off, telling me my business?"

Give that person credit for trying to help. He could be right. Listen to him. If he's all wet, don't put it that way; explain it nicely.

Maybe he wants to learn, and you'll make a friend.

A good salesman makes lots of friends, and they are among his best assets.

DECEMBER 4th

THE WRITE STUFF

A large percentage of the friction between salesmen and office is cause by that dirty word, reports.

Generally speaking, salesman are not good detail men. They dislike writing reports. Their attitude is "I could be putting in my time better selling."

But reports are important, to salesmen and the office. They are the main means of communication with headquarters, telling how you are spending the time they are paying you for.

If copies of your reports go to a distant home office, they may be their only way of knowing that you are a person, not just a pin on the territory map or a name on a payroll.

DECEMBER 5th
THE WRITE STUFF, PART 2

I knew of one salesman whose reports sold the home office on him for a district sales manager.

In fact, he wrote so well that he quit, and is now a successful newspaper columnist.

But you don't have to go that far to keep the office happy. They'll settle for short-prompt, factual reports.

DECEMBER 6th
THE WRITE STUFF, PART 3

After you've tried it for a while, writing reports becomes easier.

Just don't fight it. Figure it this way -- nobody likes to work any more than is necessary. Office personnel are that way too, and the salesman who makes them the least trouble rates high with them.

Boosters are more help than knockers. Every salesman knows that, in addition to his product, he has to sell himself. He has to be popular with people in his territory -- and his office -- to be successful.

DECEMBER 7th

AN AMERICAN CREED

On this day, when we remember the attack on Pearl Harbor, these words are appropriate:

I do not choose to be a common man. It is my right to be uncommon -- if I can.

I seek opportunity -- not security...

I want to take the calculated risk, to dream and to build, to fail and to succeed...

I will never cower before any master nor bend to any threat.

It is my heritage to stand erect, proud and unafraid; to think and act for myself;

Enjoy the benefits of my creations and to face the world boldly and say, "This I have done."

All this is what it means to be an American.

DECEMBER 8th

NO FREE LUNCH

Don't be misled into believing that somehow the world owes you a living.

The boy who believes that his parents, or the government of anyone else owes him his livelihood, and that he can collect it without labor, will wake up one day and find himself working for another boy who did not have that belief and who, therefore, earned the right to have others work for him.

DECEMBER 9th

DECISION TIME

The salesman, by the nature of his work, is exposed to the opportunity for decision-making several times a day.

If a sale is to be made, somewhere along the line a decision must be made.

The salesman should seize these daily opportunities to build his own decisiveness.

He should not only provide the facts and supporting date, but a special recommendation as to what he thinks should be done.

DECEMBER 10th

DECISION TIME, PART 2

Non-leaders do not offer decisions. They provide facts and data, but not specific recommendations that require a positive decision.

You cannot develop decisiveness without "sticking your neck out," whether it be with a customer or your boss.

If you are unwilling to do this, don't bother about any further self-development in this area -- and, parenthetically, you might as well forget about becoming a sales leader.

DECEMBER 11th

OVERCOMING OBSTACLES

It is obvious that some persons have a greater natural persistence than other, but the quality of persistence is capable of substantial development.

What is required seems to be a combination of attitudes and experience --the mental resolve not to become discouraged, plus experience in overcoming obstacles.

The man who has successfully met a major challenge has a stronger backbone for the next problem to be faced, but he must be willing to venture into difficult situations in order to get such experience.

You cannot win if you do not try. You cannot become a sales leader unless you are persistent in your effort

DECEMBER 12th

THE GROWTH OF CONFIDENCE

The development of confidence is a difficult trait to discuss. Some individuals seem to develop it gradually as they grow in experience and stature.

Others have to cross some major threshold or go through some crisis or crucible to attain it.

But confidence can be fostered; it does grow.

As with other traits, careful self-appraisal should suggest ways for building your own confidence

DECEMBER 13th
THE VALUE OF INTEGRITY

Is integrity controllable and, therefore, open to development?

Most certainly it is, assuming a man has a conscience, and we are all supposed to have one.

Breaking habits -- what the psychologists refer to as "behavior patterns" --is difficult, but it can be done.

Integrity is largely a matter of habit, of pre-conditioned behavior patterns.

An individual can develop the habit of being honest with other people, and of being brutally honest with himself.

Smiley Anders

DECEMBER 14th
HANDLING PEOPLE

Persuasiveness and the ability to handle people represent major development opportunities for most individuals; it is almost impossible to be too good in them.

The ability to handle people is so fundamental that many consider it, alone, as the key to sales leadership.

A basic knowledge of psychology and an understanding of underlying motivations is helpful.

Beyond this, there are a number of good, practical books on the subject.

DECEMBER 15th
IT'S UP TO YOU

The first principle of training and development of salespeople is "All development is self-development."

This does not mean that we are left to our own resources in using and improving our abilities.

Rather, it means that the best any company can do is provide the opportunity for development.

It can create a climate in which we can grow, give us guidance, observe our job performance, make recommendations, and perhaps provide material from time to time.

But if we don't want to acquire the necessary selling knowledge and transmute it into selling skills and habits -- well, that's that.

DECEMBER 16th
PRACTICE MAKES PERFECT

You might wonder just how you should go about developing your selling skills.

How many times have you actually practiced, out loud, one of your selling presentations?

How many times have you used a fellow salesman, or your spouse, or your image in the mirror, as the prospect and practiced your presentation?

DECEMBER 17th
SELLING AND RE-SELLING

Please take me seriously when I say that in your selling work, you'd better approach every prospect and every customer as though he'd never heard of your company or your product, and had to be sold every inch of the way.

Because that's the way your most aggressive competitor is approaching YOUR best customers -- he knows that he, too, must "sell or sink."

DECEMBER 18th

COCKY DOESN'T WORK

There is a vast difference between being self-confident and just plain overbearingly cocky.

To me one of the saddest sights in selling is the over-confident, cocky, sure-of-himself salesman who thinks he has his territory all buttoned up for the rest of his life.

Remember, the young, fresh, enthusiastic, ambitious salesman is going to fight like the devil to dislodge the self-satisfied, boom-soft competitor who thinks he got a special franchise on the business.

DECEMBER 19th

THE MINNOW THEORY

There is a type of salesman who is unsparing of his energy for prospecting, but he is fishing for minnows when he should be casting for large-mouth bass.

This is known as the small-account complex. A man devotes a great deal of time to cold-calling and tracking down leads, but he stays away from the big account.

Subconsciously, he avoids the large customer in his prospecting. Why?

The answer is simple: the big buyer is harder to sell.

The salesman knows he's going to have a tough fight and he's afraid to start slugging.

DECEMBER 20th
SELECTION PROCESS

Don't let yourself be cowered or intimidated by the buyer.

Don't even appear too grateful for the interview.

Instead, make him feel that he's been SELECTED by you; that you are giving him YOUR time.

Give him the impression that you don't pick prospects at random, but only after careful consideration.

Make him feel that he's a blue-chip choice.

DECEMBER 21st
HARRY'S METHOD

At a sales meeting, the vice president of marketing introduced a very ordinary-looking fellow, who had that year led the sales force by a large margin. The vice-president said:

"I want you to take a good look at Harry. He earned five times the average.

But is Harry five times smarter? No, I checked our personnel tests.

"Did he work five times harder? No, in fact he took more time off than most of you.

"Did Harry have a better territory? No. Did he have more education? Better health? Again, no.

"Harry is about as average as an average guy could be, except for one thing.

"The difference between Harry and the rest of you is that Harry THOUGHT five times bigger."

DECEMBER 22nd

THE VALUE OF TEAMWORK

You will not reach the top in your profession if you are not a team player.

I don't care how good you are, this truth is for you.

Cooperation is the key to success.

Whether it be playing football, selling our products or being agreeable when asked to pick up merchandise, the man who teams well will find others opening his way to his goal.

DECEMBER 23rd

ROMAN LESSON

We need a return to the importance of character, integrity and self-reliance.

It wasn't the Goths that defeated Rome -- it was the free circuses.

Luxuries, power, indulgence had made the once-tough Roman people soft. To stay popular, their emperors gave them free bread, free circuses, easier living.

So the Romans softened themselves for the ambitious, hard-working barbarians.

And in 410 A.D. the greatest nation the world had ever seen was invaded and destroyed. So beware the greedy cry of "something for nothing."

DECEMBER 24th

CHRISTMAS WISHES

We wish you for this Christmas:

A mind unafraid of mental adventure, a mind tickled by curiosity and awed by the wonder of small things; a heart that trusts beyond reason, even faith is assailed by overwhelming odds.

An abiding sense of humor, the power to see the ridiculous in life.

Work to do, work that has meaning and value both to you and others.

A consuming desire for justice tempered by mercy, a sense of responsibility leavened with lightheartedness, the grace to forgive without rancor and the humility to be forgiven without resentment.

DECEMBER 25th

'TIS THE SEASON

This is a season when heart are aglow, love abounds, and we look forward with anticipation to reunions with family and loved ones.

It is a busy time, a happy time. Let us remember that where there is peace and love, where there is cheer and laughter, the joys of Christmas will remain to last forever after.

May God's richest blessings be with you and each member of your family as you in your own way observe this Christmas season.

DECEMBER 26th

SECRET OF HAPPINESS

To awaken each morning with a smile brightening my face; to greet the day with reverence for the opportunities it contains; to approach my work with a clean mind; to hold ever before me, even in the doing of little thing, the ultimate purpose toward which I am working; to meet men and women with laughter on my lips and love in my heart; to be gentle, kind and courteous through all the hours; to approach the night with weariness that ever woos sleep and the joy that comes from work well done -- this is how I desire to waste wisely my days.

DECEMBER 27th

THOUGHTS OF THE SEASON

A Christian who has deep faith in Jesus Christ and who lives this faith, acquires through the passing of years a true wisdom: Wisdom to know in what direction to lead his life, wisdom to have a vision about what is important, wisdom to have enough endurance to accept the hardships and trials of authentic Christian living.

In these challenging times our Lord is telling us that we will find happiness and salvation not by violence, not in vehement passion, not by renouncing our faith, but by enduring patiently.

This is the wisdom that Jesus gives us today and for the new year.

And this is the sincere wish I extend to you.

DECEMBER 28th

HAPPINESS AND HOPE

Man is made for happiness, and yet he is unhappy. On this earth his hopes are never completely fulfilled.

We are forced to conclude that the flesh -- the body -- is not the fountainhead of happiness. Nor is power or knowledge of even man himself.

We must look elsewhere to find the source and the object of happiness.

The virtue of hope points us toward the goal of perfect happiness -- total union with God through knowledge and love.

Filled with the virtue of hope, we are able to separate from one another those things that bring us fleeting pleasures or enjoyment and the things that bring us at least a glimpse of true happiness.

DECEMBER 29th

A NEW YEAR'S PRAYER

Three weeks after the attack on Pearl Harbor, President Franklin D. Roosevelt asked the nation to set aside New Year's Day as a day of prayer for divine guidance.

An editorial appeared in the Jan. 2, 1942 issue of U.S. News & World Report magazine, titled "A New Year's Prayer."

It began:

Some of us have not prayed before. Some of us think it soft and sentimental, remote and intangible.

Some of us have prayed again and again, and the world grows no better -- the forces of evil spread their terror even farther to the four corners of the earth.

But we come back to prayer just the same because an abiding instinct bids us to grope further...

DECEMBER 30th

A NEW YEAR'S PRAYER, PART 2

It is natural to pray for victory. But victory over whom and over what?

Shall we merely ask that the power of almighty God be visited on those who attack us so that we may emerge triumphant?

Surely prayer for strength just to destroy other human being makes little sense by itself...

We pray to almighty God for help -- maybe the first help we can expect will come when we begin to help ourselves -- to help subdue the maelstrom of human currents and cross-currents that drive millions of us into conflict every day, not necessarily in the wars of organized murder but in the battles of everyday life...

DECEMBER 31st

A NEW YEAR'S PRAYER, PART 3

Let us pray to almighty God to raise us from this level of material conflict to something different -- something higher, something more powerful.

Let us pray for a strengthening of our sense of reason.

We must contrive to reach the hearts of our fellow men, irrespective of race, creed or color...so that, across the no-man's land of human distress, understanding hearts will speak to understanding hearts...

SPECIAL DAYS: THOUGHTS FROM HOLIDAYS, MILESTONE EVENTS IN LIFE:

THE AMERICAN REVOLUTION WANTS YOU TO JOIN IT:

THIS YEAR MARKS THE BIRTHDAY OF THE UNITED STATES OF AMERICA. THE 200th BIRTHDAY OF A NATION AND A SYSTEM THAT HOLDS AS HIGH A PROMISE TODAY AS IT DID WHEN THE FOUNDING FATHERS GAVE IT LIFE...

THE AMERICAN REVOLUTION IS A LIVING THING. WE - YOU, ME, ALL OF US - CAN SHAPE THE AMERICAN REVOLUTION TO MEANINGS OTHER THAN IT HAD FOR OUR FOREFATHERS. WE CAN JOIN IT RIGHT AND MAKE THE AMERICAN REVOLUTION SOMETHING OF DEEP MEANING TO EACH OF US INDIVIDUALLY, OF TO THE NATION AS A WHOLE...

CHRISTMAS GIFTS:

WE WISH YOU FOR 1978:

...A MIND UNAFRAID OF MENTAL ADVENTURE, A MIND TICKLED BY CURIOSITY AND AWED BY THE WONDER OF SMALL THINGS; A HEART THAT TRUSTS BEYOND REASON, EVEN WHEN FAITH IS ASSAILED BY OVERWHELMING ODDS.

WE WISH YOU:

...AN ABIDING SENSE OF HUMOR, THE POWER TO SEE THE RIDICULOUS IN LIFE...

WE WISH YOU:

... WORK TO DO, WORK THAT HAS MEANING AND VALUE BOTH TO YOU AND OTHERS...

WE WISH YOU:

A CONSUMING DESIRE FOR JUSTICE TEMPERED BY MERCY, A SENSE OF RESPONSIBILITY LEAVENED WITH LIGHTHEARTEDNESS, THE GRACE TO FORGIVE WITHOUT RANCOR AND THE HUMILITY TO BE FORGIVEN WITHOUT RESENTMENT.

THE NEW YEAR:

IN THESE CHALLENGING TIMES OUR LORD IS TELLING US THAT WE WILL FIND HAPPINESS AND SALVATION NOT BY VIOLENCE, NOT IN VEHEMENT PASSION, NOT BY RENOUNCING OUR FAITH, BUT BY ENDURING PATIENTLY. THIS IS THE WISDOM THAT JESUS GIVES US TODAY FOR THE NEW YEAR. AND THIS IS THE SINCERE WISH I EXTEND TO YOU...

A 75th BIRTHDAY PRAYER:

LORD, YOU KNOW I AM GROWING OLDER. KEEP ME FROM BECOMING TALKATIVE AND POSSESSED WITH THE IDEA THAT I MUST EXPRESS MYSELF ON EVERY SUBJECT ... WITH MY VAST STORE OF WISDOM, IT DOES SEEM A

PITY NOT TO USE IT. BUT YOU KNOW, LORD, THAT I WANT A FEW FRIENDS IN THE END. AMEN.

ABOUT THE AUTHOR

From Bunkie to Baton Rouge, from Aggies to Cajuns, Smiley Anders reaps the harvest of Louisiana humor and sets it on the table for his readers six days a week. This, his first book, features excerpts from some of his best columns 1979-1990

For more than 25 years Smiley Anders has been writing his six-days-a-week column for The Advocate in Baton Rouge, La. The column has received three first place awards from the National Society of Newspaper Columnists (in 1985, 1996 and 2004) in the items category. In 1997 the name of the category was changed to the Herb Caen Award to honor the San Francisco Chronicle''s long-time items columnist.

Smiley (yes, that is his "real" name) started the column after a 13-year career in business journalism, and was The Advocate''s business reporter before becoming a columnist. For his business reporting, he was named the first "Communicator of the Year" in 1975 by the Public Relations Association of Louisiana.

A native of Natchez, Miss., he received B.A. and M.A. degrees in journalism from Louisiana State University. He and his wife Katherine live in a 1922 home in Spanish Town, Baton Rouge's oldest neighborhood.

www.ingramcontent.com/pod-product-compliance
Lightning Source LLC
Chambersburg PA
CBHW031837170526
45157CB00001B/337